STECK-VAUGHN SOCIAL STUDIES

Regions of Our Country

Level D

PROGRAM CONSULTANTS

Sonya Abbye Taylor, Senior Associate
Professional Development Network, Inc.
(Education Consultant)
New Rochelle, N.Y.
and
Field Supervisor and Instructor
Manhattanville College
Purchase, N.Y.

Barbara C. Donahue, Principal
Burlington County Special Services School District
Westampton, N.J.

STECK-VAUGHN
ELEMENTARY · SECONDARY · ADULT · LIBRARY

A Harcourt Company

www.steck-vaughn.com

Executive Editor: Diane Sharpe
Project Editor: Janet Jerzycki
Assistant Art Director: Cynthia Ellis
Design Manager: John J. Harrison
Photo Editor: Margie Foster
Cover Design and Illustration: D. Childress
Program Development, Design, Illustration,
    and Production: Proof Positive/Farrowlyne Associates, Inc.

ACKNOWLEDGMENTS

Photo Credits: Cover © James Randklev/Tony Stone Images; p.5 © Superstock; p.6 © Richard Hutchings; p.8 Superstock; p.10 © Russ Kinne/Photo Researchers; p.12 Vermont Agency of Development & Community Affairs; p.14 NOAA/NESDIS/NCDC/SDSD; p.16 © Michal Heron; p.17 Jamestown Festival Park; p.18 The John Hancock Mutual Life Insurance Company; p.19 George Eastman House; p.20 © Rhoda Sidney/Image Works; p.21 © Glenn Hoffman/Puerto Rico Tourism Company; p.23 © Michal Heron; p.25 © Paolo Koch/Photo Researchers; p.26 © Michal Heron; p.27 (top right) © Tom Hollyman/Photo Researchers, (middle right) © Joan Menschenfreund; p.29 The Bettmann Archive; p.33 © Kunio Owaki/The Stock Market; p.35 © J. Barnell/Superstock; p.37 © Jon Riley/Tony Stone Images; p.42 © Joan Menschenfreund; p.43 © Kunio Owaki/The Stock Market; p.44 (top left) © Grant Heilman/Grant Heilman Photography; p.45 WNBC-TV; p.46 Courtesy L. L. Bean Company; p.47 © John Elk/Tony Stone Images; p.53 © Kunio Owaki/The Stock Market; p.57 (top right) © Michal Heron, (middle right) © David R. Frazier/Tony Stone Images; p.58 © A. Topping/Photo Researchers; p.60 Colonial Williamsburg Foundation; p.61 © Michael Philip Manheim/Photo Researchers; p.62 (top) © Julie Houck/Stock Boston, (left) © Eric Kroll/Taurus Photos; p.63 (top right) © Michal Heron, (bottom) Chuck O'Rear; p.64 © Uniphoto; p.66 (middle left) Florida Department of Commerce, Division of Tourism, (bottom); p.67 UPI/Bettmann; p.73 © John M. Roberts/The Stock Market; p.77 © Superstock; p.78 © Oliver Benn/Tony Stone Images; p.82 © Don Smetzer/Tony Stone Images; p.83 (top right) © Andre Jenny/Unicorn Stock Photos, (bottom) © Paul Meredith/Tony Stone Images; p.84 © Alan Pitcairn/Grant Heilman Photography; p.85 Courtesy Chrysler Corporation; p.86 (top left)© Superstock, (bottom) © Jeff Greenberg/Unicorn Stock Photos; p.87 Chicago Historical Society; p.97 (top) © Superstock, (right) © Joe Munro/Photo Researchers; p.98 © N. H. Cheatham/Photo Researchers; p.102 © Susan McCartney/Photo Researchers; p.103 Colorado Department of Public Relations; p.104 © George Hall/Woodfin Camp Associates; p.105 © Martin Weaver/Woodfin Camp Associates; p.106 (top) © L. L. T. Rhodes/Taurus Photos, (left); p.107 The Bettmann Archive; p.112 © Superstock; p.115 (top right) © Craig Wells/Tony Stone Images, (bottom)© Bob Thomason/Tony Stone Images; p.120 © Gamma-Liaison; p.121 © Adam Woolfitt/Woodfine Camp Associates; p.122 © Superstock; p.123 © J. Pat Carter/Gamma-Liaison; p.124 © Fred W. Marvel/Oklahoma Tourism; p.125 © R. Jacques/Photo Researchers; p.126 Courtesy Shell Oil Company; p.132 © Cliff Hallenbeck/Tony Stone Images; p.135 (top right) © Cindy Charles/PhotoEdit, (bottom) Courtesy Wells Fargo Bank; p.137 (top right) © H. Kinne/Photo Researchers; p.139 (top right); p.142 The Granger Collection; p.144 © Gus Boyd/Photo Researchers; p.145 © Audrey Sandin/Tony Stone Images; p.146 (top) © Joe Rychetnik/Photo Researchers, (left) © Michal Heron; p.147 © Joan Menschenfreund; p.148 (top left) © The Image Works, (top right) © Grant Heilman/Grant Heilman Photography, (middle left) © James Wilson/Gamma-Liaison; p.149 © Nancy Crampton.

ISBN: 0-8172-6553-8

12 13 14 085 05 04 03

Contents

Our Nation, The United States

You are a member of your family, your neighborhood, and your community. You are part of something else, too. You are an American. You live in the United States of America.

Unit 1 of this book will help you find answers to questions like these about our nation.

- What is the land in the United States like?
- Where do Americans come from?
- How do Americans live?

UNIT PROJECT

Start a team project. Find another class in another part of the United States. Use a computer if you can. Become pen pals by writing to those students. Find out what life is like where they live. Work on your project as you read Unit 1.

A Large and Varied Land

The flag of the United States has one star for each state. How many stars are there?

Where is the United States? What does it look like? How hot or cold is it? These are questions about the **geography** of the United States. Geography is the study of Earth and how we live on it.

Where Is the United States?

The United States is on the **continent** of North America. A continent is a large body of land. The map on page 7 shows North America and the countries that are part of it.

 Find the United States on the map. Write *U.S.* next to the United States. *U.S.* is the abbreviation for United States.

Look at the map again. The United States looks like a puzzle with many pieces. These pieces are called states. There are 50 states. *United* means together. The name of our country, the United States, means 50 states together.

Forty-eight states are in the part of our country that lies between Canada and Mexico. Each state touches at least one other state. Look at the map key. The dotted lines you see on the map stand for **borders.** Borders separate the states.

 Look at the compass rose on the map on page 7. The letters <u>N</u>, <u>S</u>, <u>E</u>, and <u>W</u> stand for the four cardinal directions. They are North, South, East, and West. Put a ✔ on the country that is south of the United States.

Two states do not touch any other state.
They are Alaska and Hawaii. Hawaii is about
2,400 miles away in the Pacific Ocean.

 Find Alaska on the map. What direction is Alaska from Mexico? Write your answer here.

_____

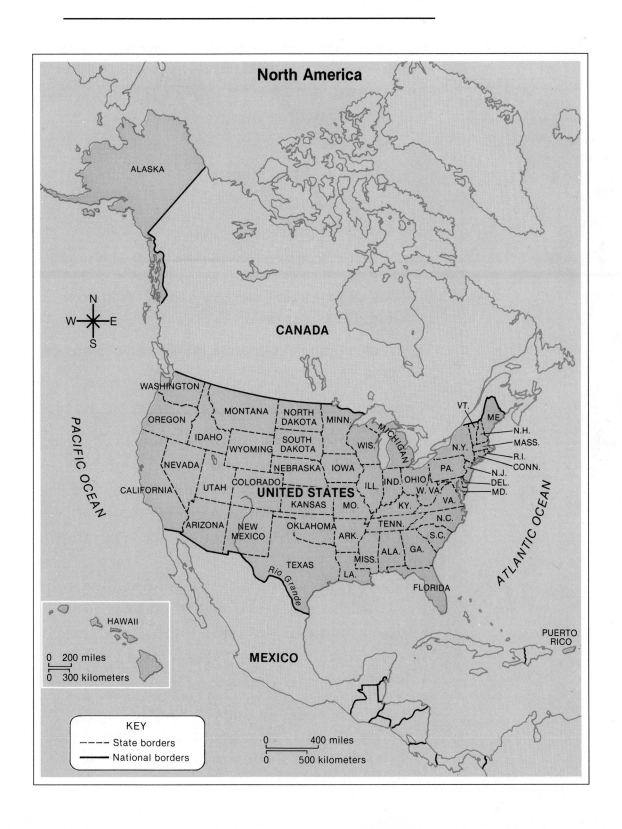

North America

ALASKA

CANADA

N
W E
S

WASHINGTON
OREGON
IDAHO
MONTANA
NORTH DAKOTA
SOUTH DAKOTA
WYOMING
NEVADA
NEBRASKA
UTAH
COLORADO
CALIFORNIA
KANSAS
MINN.
WIS.
MICHIGAN
IOWA
ILL. IND. OHIO
MO.
UNITED STATES
ARIZONA
NEW MEXICO
OKLAHOMA
ARK.
TEXAS
LA.
MISS.
ALA. GA.
TENN.
KY.
W. VA.
VA.
N.C.
S.C.
PA.
VT.
ME.
N.H.
MASS.
R.I.
CONN.
N.Y.
N.J.
DEL.
MD.
FLORIDA

PACIFIC OCEAN

ATLANTIC OCEAN

Rio Grande

HAWAII

0 200 miles
0 300 kilometers

MEXICO

PUERTO RICO

KEY
- - - State borders
— National borders

0 400 miles
0 500 kilometers

7

Regions of the United States

The United States is a very large country. In fact, it's the fourth largest country in the world. Our nation stretches 2,807 miles from the East Coast to the West Coast. And then there are Alaska and Hawaii, too! How can you study something so big?

One way to study this big nation is to divide it into areas called **regions.** The United States can be divided into six different regions:

- Northeast Region
- Southeast Region
- North Central Region
- Rocky Mountain Region
- Southwest Region
- Pacific Region

 Look at the region map on page 9. Find your state. Put a star on it.

What region is your state in? Write your answer here.

_____

Each region has something special about it. Some have lots of mountains, and some are very flat. Some regions get lots of rain, and some are very dry. Some regions are warm most of the year. Some regions get very cold in winter.

The regions of the United States can also be alike. Children in every region go to school. We watch many of the same television shows. We eat many of the same foods. And we do many of the same jobs.

 Look at the map on page 9. Find the region where you live. Color your region. Then choose five colors and shade the remaining five regions on the region map.

These boys walk to school in a snowy region.

8

What do you think is one thing that makes your region special? Tell why. Write your answers here.

_____

_____

_____

The States in Each Region

The Pacific Region
Alaska, Hawaii Washington, Oregon, California

The North Central Region
North Dakota, South Dakota, Nebraska, Indiana, Michigan, Wisconsin, Missouri, Kansas, Iowa, Illinois, Ohio, Minnesota

The Northeast Region
Maine, New Hampshire, Vermont, Massachusetts, Connecticut, Rhode Island, New York, New Jersey, Pennsylvania, Delaware, Maryland

The Rocky Mountain Region
Montana, Wyoming, Colorado, Idaho, Utah, Nevada

The Southwest Region
Texas, Oklahoma, New Mexico, Arizona

The Southeast Region
Virginia, West Virginia, North Carolina, South Carolina, Georgia, Kentucky, Tennessee, Alabama, Mississippi, Florida, Louisiana, Arkansas

The Land of the United States

In some ways the land of the United States is like a giant roller coaster. A **relief map** shows where the land is high and where it is low. It can also show the shapes and names of rivers, lakes, and mountains. A relief map is a **special-purpose map.** That means that the map gives special facts about just one topic.

 Look at the relief map on page 11. The shaded areas are mountains. What part of the country has more mountains, the East or the West? Write your answer here.

_____

Mountains and hills and other shapes of the land are called **landforms.** The land along the ocean is a landform. It is called a **coast.** The coast along the Atlantic Ocean is a coastal **plain.** A plain is a low, flat area of land.

 Look at the relief map key on page 11. Find the color for plains. Find the plain that is on the east coast of the United States. Mark an X on that plain. That X is the starting point for your roller coaster ride across the United States!

After the coastal plains, you slowly climb the Appalachian Mountains. Find the Appalachian Mountains on the map on page 11. Mark M on the mountains.

On the other side of the mountains are the plateaus. Plateaus are high, flat areas of land. Look at the map. Find the plateau near the Arkansas River. Put a P there.

The roller coaster is zooming across the flat Great Plains. Get ready to climb the Rocky Mountains. They are some of the tallest mountains in the United States!

 Mark another M on the Rocky Mountains.

Miles of wheat cover the Great Plains of the United States.

Plateau

Next, you speed down the mountains and across a plateau. After the plateau, you climb more mountains until . . . splash! You're in the ocean!

 Write the name of the ocean here.

_____

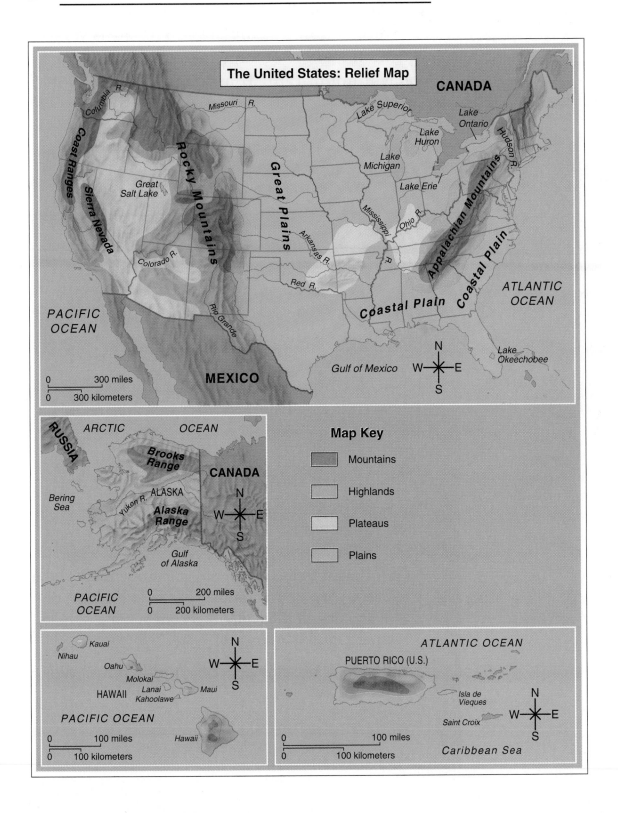

The United States: Relief Map

CANADA

Columbia R.

Missouri R.

Lake Superior

Lake Ontario

Lake Huron

Hudson R.

Coast Ranges

Rocky Mountains

Great Salt Lake

Sierra Nevada

Lake Michigan

Great Plains

Lake Erie

Appalachian Mountains

Mississippi

Ohio R.

Coastal Plain

Arkansas R.

Colorado R.

ATLANTIC OCEAN

Red R.

PACIFIC OCEAN

Coastal Plain

Rio Grande

MEXICO

Gulf of Mexico

Lake Okeechobee

0   300 miles

0   300 kilometers

RUSSIA

ARCTIC   OCEAN

Brooks Range

CANADA

Bering Sea

Yukon R.

ALASKA

Alaska Range

Gulf of Alaska

PACIFIC OCEAN

0   200 miles

0   200 kilometers

Map Key

Mountains

Highlands

Plateaus

Plains

Kauai

Nihau

Oahu

Molokai

Lanai

Kahoolawe

Maui

HAWAII

Hawaii

PACIFIC OCEAN

0   100 miles

0   100 kilometers

ATLANTIC OCEAN

PUERTO RICO (U.S.)

Isla de Vieques

Saint Croix

Caribbean Sea

0   100 miles

0   100 kilometers

Climates of the United States

"Wow, it's hot today." "What a storm we had last night!" When you say things like these, you're talking about the **weather.** Weather is made up of several things. Two of these are **temperature** and **moisture.**

Temperature is how hot or cold the air is. Moisture is how wet the air is. The air is very wet when it rains or snows. Weather changes. Today it might rain. Tomorrow it may be hot and dry.

 What two things are part of the weather? Write your answer here.

_____

_____

These two people have stopped to enjoy the view from a mountain in the Northeast.

If you say "The summers are _always_ very hot where I live," you're talking about the **climate.** The climate is the kind of weather an area has year after year.

You can find out what the weather will be like each day by listening to a weather report. But if you want to find out what the weather will be like all year, you look at a **climate map.** A climate map shows the climate in different areas. Within each area the climate is very much the same.

 The United States has many climates. Look at the climate map key on page 13. Circle the part of the country that usually has cool summers, mild winters, and is often wet.

What kind of summers does Alaska have? Write your answer here.

_____

_____

UNIT
PROJECT
Tip

Write to your pen pals. Tell them about your region. Write about the landforms, climate, and weather in your region. Ask them what is special about their region. Do they have lots of mountains? Is it very rainy? How is their region different from yours? How is it the same?

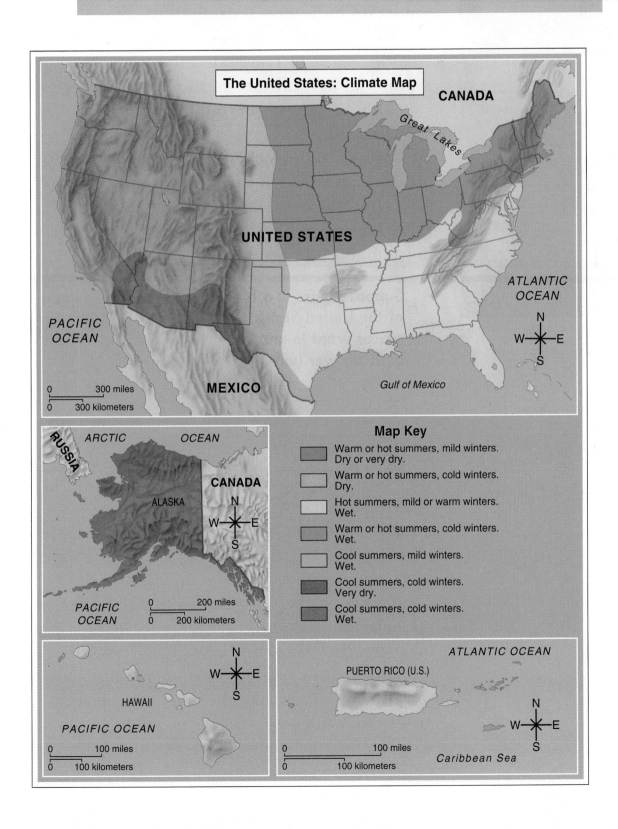

The United States: Climate Map

CANADA

Great Lakes

UNITED STATES

ATLANTIC OCEAN

PACIFIC OCEAN

N
W—E
S

0   300 miles
0   300 kilometers

MEXICO

Gulf of Mexico

ARCTIC   OCEAN

RUSSIA

CANADA

ALASKA

N
W—E
S

PACIFIC OCEAN

0   200 miles
0   200 kilometers

Map Key

Warm or hot summers, mild winters. Dry or very dry.

Warm or hot summers, cold winters. Dry.

Hot summers, mild or warm winters. Wet.

Warm or hot summers, cold winters. Wet.

Cool summers, mild winters. Wet.

Cool summers, cold winters. Very dry.

Cool summers, cold winters. Wet.

N
W—E
S

HAWAII

PACIFIC OCEAN

0   100 miles
0   100 kilometers

ATLANTIC OCEAN

PUERTO RICO (U.S.)

N
W—E
S

0   100 miles
0   100 kilometers

Caribbean Sea

Weather Reports

Weather satellites take pictures like this of clouds high above Earth.

What's the weather like today? Lots of people found out by listening to a weather report on radio or television.

The information comes from the National Weather Service. The Service has weather stations all around the country. The stations check the weather every hour and send reports to Washington, D.C.

Weather stations check temperatures. They measure moisture in the air. If there is rain or snow, they measure how much is falling. If there is a storm, they find out which way it is moving and how fast it is going.

 Suppose there is a big snowstorm in the middle of the United States. Why would people in other places want to know where it is moving? Write your answer here.

_____

_____

_____

The National Weather Service also has weather **satellites.** Satellites are sent into space to take photographs of Earth. Then the Service can see where storms are going. Radios in the satellites send the information to Earth. People use computers to examine the information and make weather maps and reports.

People who study the weather are not always sure what it will be like. But they can **predict,** or tell what will _probably_ happen. The National Weather Service shares its predictions with radio and television stations.

CHAPTER CHECKUP

Complete each sentence. Circle the letter in front of the correct answer.

1. The United States has

   a. 13 states.

   b. 48 states.

   c. 52 states.

   d. 50 states.

2. Borders separate

   a. continents.

   b. landforms.

   c. plains.

   d. states and countries.

3. A region of the United States is

   a. the study of Earth's land.

   b. a large country.

   c. a group of states.

   d. a kind of weather.

4. A relief map shows

   a. climate areas.

   b. state borders.

   c. where the land is high and low.

   d. rivers only.

5. The land along the Atlantic Ocean is

   a. flat coastal plain.

   b. high plateaus.

   c. the Rocky Mountains.

   d. Alaska.

6. A plateau is

   a. low land along the ocean.

   b. a tall mountain.

   c. high, flat land.

   d. a small island.

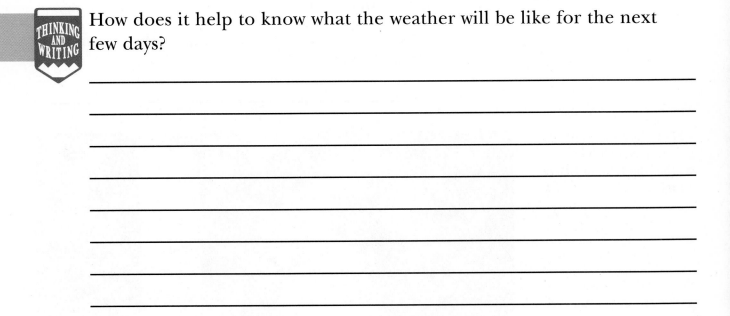

THINKING AND WRITING

How does it help to know what the weather will be like for the next few days?

_____

_____

_____

_____

_____

_____

_____

_____

CHAPTER 2

Who Is an American?

Each person who lives in the United States is special in some way. We all live and work together in the United States. We are part of a special group—the American people.

The First Americans

The first people to live in the United States were American Indians, or **Native Americans.** *Native* means the first people to live in a place. American Indians came from Asia to Alaska thousands of years ago. Over time, they settled all over North and South America.

The American Indians formed hundreds of different groups. Some groups of American Indians lived in small villages and planted crops such as squash, beans, and corn. Other groups traveled to find food and never stayed in one place for very long.

 How did American Indians get to North and South America?

A Navajo girl learns an old skill. Her grandmother teaches her how to weave a rug.

New Americans

The first explorers of North America were Vikings. They sailed from Greenland to North America about 1,000 years ago. They did not stay in North America. People in Europe, Asia, and Africa did not know that the Vikings had explored North America.

About 500 years after the Viking explorers, Christopher Columbus sailed west from Europe. He landed on an island between North and South America in 1492. Soon other explorers came from Europe.

Later, families from Europe started moving to North America, too. They began **colonies**. A colony is a group of people ruled by another country. The people living in the colonies had to work hard. These **colonists** built homes, farmed, and started businesses.

Homes in the early colonies looked like these homes. They were made of mud on sticks.

Look at the picture graph below. Sometimes it is easier to understand numbers if you see them as pictures. This graph uses symbols for numbers. This picture graph shows how the colonies grew. How many colonists were there in 1680? How many were there in 1740, 60 years later? Write your answers here.

1680: _____ 1740: _____

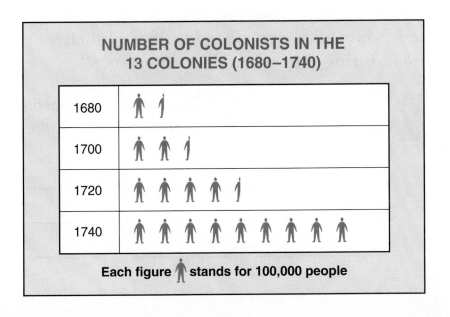

New Americans Meet the First Americans

The colonists had come from farms, towns, and cities in Europe. North America was a wilderness area. The colonists had to learn new skills to live in North America. At first, most American Indians were friendly toward the colonists. American Indians taught the colonists about foods they could grow. From Europe, the colonists brought metal tools, guns, cattle, and horses. The American Indians had never seen such things before.

How did American Indians help the colonists?

_____

_____

_____

American Indians wanted to keep living on the land their people had lived on for hundreds of years. The colonists wanted to explore and use the land. They also wanted to build the kinds of towns and farms they remembered from Europe. American Indians and colonists fought many battles about land. The colonists fought with guns. The American Indians used spears and bows and arrows to fight the battles. Because their weapons were less powerful, many more American Indians died during the battles than colonists.

Why did the American Indians and the European colonists fight about how to use the land? Write your answer here.

_____

_____

_____

The Pilgrims were early colonists who learned skills from American Indians.

More New Americans Arrive

Beginning in the 1600s, some Africans were forced to come to this country. These people were sold to colonists as **slaves.** A slave is a person who is owned by another person. Some colonists used slaves to do the hard work on the farms and in the new towns.

In 1861 Americans fought one another in the Civil War. After the war slaves became free. New laws said that no person could ever be made a slave in the United States again.

During the 1700s and 1800s, many **immigrants** from Europe came to the United States. Immigrants are people who come from one country to live in another country. They wanted a chance to own land or find good jobs.

Today the largest numbers of immigrants come from Asia and Latin America. Today's immigrants, like immigrants of earlier times, hope to find a better life.

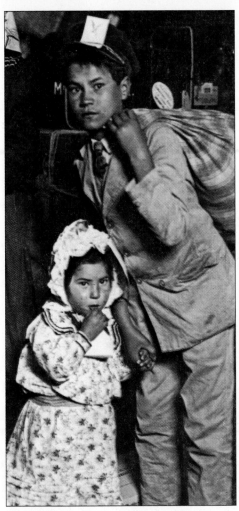

These children from Italy arrived in New York City with their family about 100 years ago.

■ **A bar graph uses bars to stand for numbers. The bar graph below shows the countries that many immigrants came from between 1820 and 1950. Circle the name of the country the most immigrants came from.**

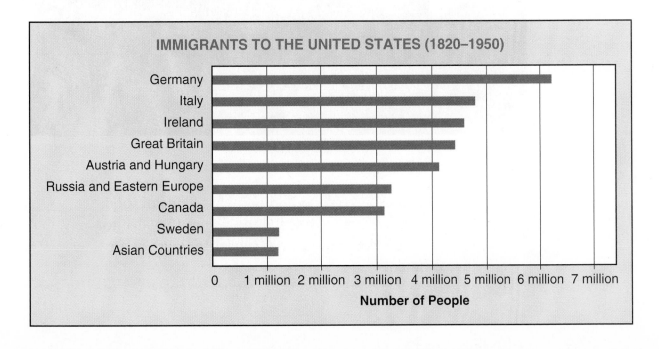

IMMIGRANTS TO THE UNITED STATES (1820–1950)

Germany
Italy
Ireland
Great Britain
Austria and Hungary
Russia and Eastern Europe
Canada
Sweden
Asian Countries

0   1 million 2 million 3 million 4 million 5 million 6 million 7 million

Number of People

19

Americans Living Together

North Americans have many different backgrounds. Most Americans speak English, but some speak other languages, such as Spanish, Chinese, or Korean. In fact, many words you use each day come from other languages! Did you know that *banana* and *zebra* come from African languages? *Tomato* and *chipmunk* come from American Indian languages!

Although Americans are different in many ways, they are a lot alike. Many Americans enjoy the same foods, such as peanut butter and corn on the cob. Americans do many of the same things, such as play baseball and visit friends. Most important, Americans share the same home, the United States of America.

Many different kinds of people live in the United States of America.

UNIT
PROJECT
Tip

Write to your pen pals to find out what kinds of food they like. Ask them to describe the games they like to play. Are their food and games similar to yours or are they different?

Did you know that about $3\frac{1}{2}$ million Americans live on an island in the Atlantic Ocean? They live in Puerto Rico. Puerto Rico is part of the United States, but it is not a state.

Columbus landed on Puerto Rico in 1493. He made it a Spanish colony. For about 400 years, Puerto Rico belonged to Spain. Then in 1898, after a war, Puerto Rico became part of the United States.

Most people in Puerto Rico speak Spanish. Students learn English in school. Most people live in cities and work in factories, businesses, or for the government. Outside the cities, some people raise cattle. Farmers grow crops such as sugar, coffee, bananas, and pineapples.

Puerto Rico has a pleasant climate, many beautiful beaches, and mountains that bring many visitors to the island!

 Look at the map to the right. Find Puerto Rico. Draw a circle around it.

Find Culebra and Vieques islands on the relief map. They're part of Puerto Rico, too.

 Water surrounds Puerto Rico. Write the name of the body of water to the south of Puerto Rico.

_____

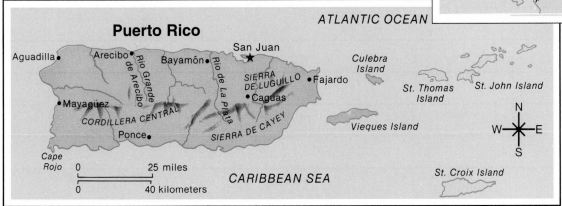

CHAPTER ✓ CHECKUP

Complete each sentence. Circle the letter in front of the correct answer.

1. The first Americans were

   a. American Indians.
   b. Puerto Ricans.
   c. African Americans.
   d. Europeans.

2. A colony is

   a. an early American Indian farm.
   b. a place discovered by Columbus.
   c. a group of people ruled by another country.
   d. where African Americans originally came from.

3. From Europe, the early colonists brought metal tools, guns, cattle and

   a. bows and arrows.
   b. horses.
   c. Vikings.
   d. spears.

4. Long ago, some Africans were forced to come to this country as

   a. colonists.
   b. slaves.
   c. settlers.
   d. U.S. citizens.

5. Immigrants are

   a. people who are owned by another person.
   b. people who come from one country to live in another country.
   c. the first Americans.
   d. people looking for jobs.

6. Americans come from

   a. many different countries.
   b. Mexico only.
   c. England only.
   d. Africa only.

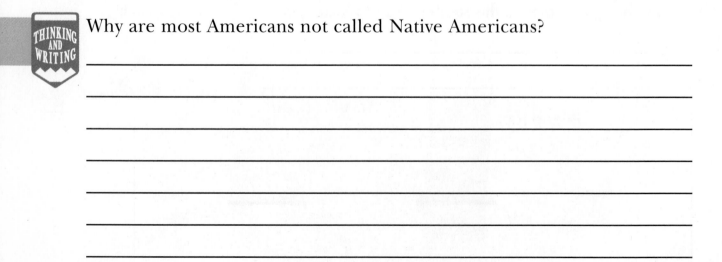

THINKING AND WRITING Why are most Americans not called Native Americans?

_____

_____

_____

_____

_____

_____

How Do Americans Live Together?

In the last chapter you read about the many kinds of people who have come to live in the United States. Did you wonder how so many different people can live in one country?

Our Nation's Leaders

It isn't easy for people with different ideas to work and live together. Imagine how hard it would be to drive a car if everyone did what he or she wanted to do. Some people might drive on the right and some might drive on the left. Some people might even drive on the sidewalks. That's why we have rules to tell drivers where they can drive.

Write one thing that might happen if there were no rules for people who drive cars. Write your answer here.

_____

_____

Bicycles can be dangerous, too. The police officer is telling students about rules for riding bicycles.

Towns, states, and nations need rules, too. Who makes these rules? Groups of people called **governments** do. Rules made by governments are called **laws.** Governments also make sure that the laws are obeyed. We have governments for our towns, our states, and our nation.

A town or city government is called a **local government.** Local governments provide **services** like the police, who work to help and protect us.

 Look at the picture below. Local governments provide this service. Write the reason why this service is important to you.

_____

_____

Your state government provides services for all the communities in your state. It builds roads between cities. It makes laws about what people can and cannot do in the state.

The government of the United States also makes laws and provides services. For example, it helps maintain highways between states.

Firefighting is a local service. Firefighters must be near homes and businesses.

24

The United States is a **democracy.** That means that the people who live here can **vote** for, or choose, the people in their governments. The people who live in a town vote for the **mayor** of the town. The mayor is the person who leads the town.

The people who live in a state vote for the **governor.** The governor is the person who leads the state. The person who leads the whole country is called the **President.** Everyone who is 18 or older can vote to choose the President.

Circle the name of the person who leads the United States.

mayor   governor   President

The President leads the country but does not make the laws. The people who make the country's laws are in **Congress.** Congress has two parts: the **Senate** and the **House of Representatives.**

The people of each state vote for two senators. They also vote for the representatives. The more people there are in a state, the more representatives the state has. Vermont has very few people, so it has only one representative. California has lots of people, so it has 52 representatives.

It is very hard to lead a town, state, or country. It is also hard to make good laws. That is why people have to be very careful when they vote. We must try to pick the best people to be our leaders.

If you were in Congress, what law would you like to make? Write it here.

_____

_____

The senators and representatives from each state make laws in this building in Washington, D.C.

Building a Nation

People still make some things by hand. This girl is learning how to make a patchwork quilt.

For hundreds of years, people in the United States have worked hard to build homes and businesses.

Farming has always been important. Many American Indians and colonists were farmers. Today American farms grow food for people in the United States and other countries.

Americans also make a lot of goods. American Indians and early colonists made their own goods by hand. In the late 1700s, Americans began making goods in factories.

The way Americans work today is very different from colonial times. Americans have all kinds of jobs. The bar graph on this page shows different job groupings. It also shows how many people work in each job grouping. Today, the **service job** grouping has the largest number of people. People who have service jobs do not *make* anything. People who have service jobs *do* something to help other people. Service workers might give you a haircut, serve you food, or clean your teeth.

Look at the bar graph. Which job grouping has about twice as many workers as the manufacturing grouping?

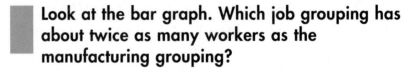

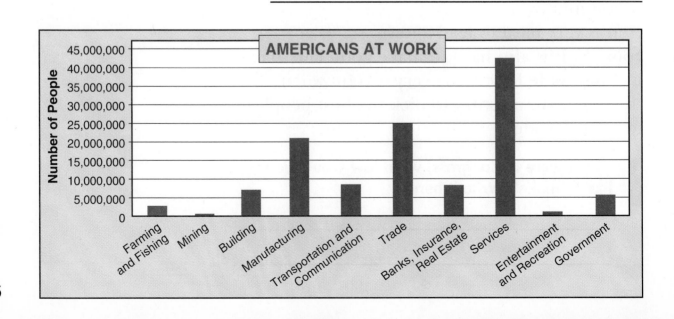

Our Natural Resources

The United States is rich in **natural resources.** Natural resources have helped make our country great. A natural resource is something from nature that we use.

One of the most important resources of the United States is soil. Soil is used to grow crops. Water is another important resource. You probably never realized how important water is. It's so easy to get a glass of water. But if we didn't have much water, we couldn't grow enough food.

 Write two ways you use water.

_____

_____

Water is useful for other things, too. We use our lakes and rivers to get to places and to move things. Many of our crops and products travel on ships. We also use the power of moving water to make electricity.

When the colonists came from Europe there were many natural resources. Most people thought the United States had more than enough natural resources. Today we know that some resources will not last forever.

Minerals are one kind of resource that will not last. **Minerals** are materials that are produced by nature, such as iron and coal.

Trees and water are two important resources.

Minerals are usually dug up from the earth. We use iron to make steel. Buildings and cars are made out of steel. We can **recycle** some items made out of minerals, such as steel and aluminum cans. When we recycle, we reuse resources. Reusing resources helps keep us from running out of those resources.

Trees are another great resource. We use them to build homes and furniture. Paper is also made from trees. Before the colonists came, there were forests all over North America. Many forests have been cut down since then. Luckily, trees can be replanted. We have to be careful how many trees we use because trees take a long time to grow.

People can save trees by recycling paper. By recycling paper, we reuse the paper and do not have to cut down as many trees.

 What do we know today about natural resources that the colonists didn't know?

_____

_____

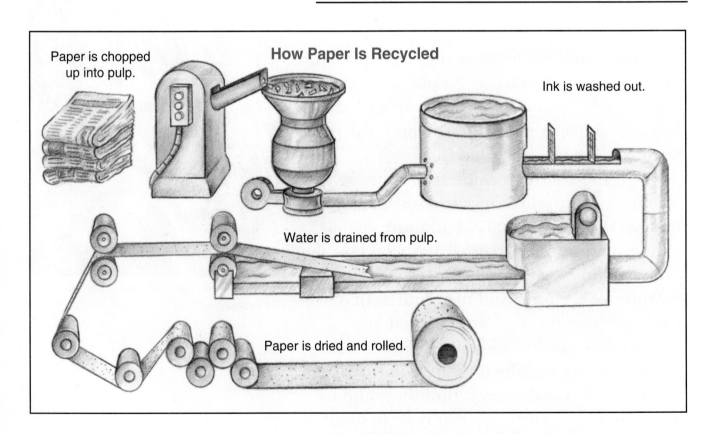

How Paper Is Recycled

Paper is chopped up into pulp.

Ink is washed out.

Water is drained from pulp.

Paper is dried and rolled.

UNIT PROJECT Tip

Write to your pen pals and ask them to describe their community. How do people use the natural resources in their area? What do people in their community do to protect their resources?

You have read about one important natural resource—our forests. You know that we need trees in order to make many of the goods we want and need. But did you know that trees help clean the air and help save water?

What would happen if we cut down all our forests? What would happen to the plants and animals that live in the forests? A man named John Muir asked those questions 100 years ago.

 What do you think could happen if we want too many goods made from trees?

_____

_____

John Muir

John Muir was born in Scotland. He was about your age when his family moved to the United States. For 40 years Muir lived in the forests all over the world. He saw what happened when people cut down thousands of trees. The land was left bare and ruined.

Muir decided to do something to protect the forests. He started the Sierra Club, a group that protects forests and other lands. He got Congress to make some of the most beautiful forests into national parks so everyone could go to see them.

Today, we have laws that help keep our air and water clean. The Endangered Species Act is one law that makes it illegal to harm certain wild animals. The law also protects the forests and other areas where those animals live. If we don't protect our resources, we may not have any in the future.

CHAPTER CHECKUP

Complete each sentence. Circle the letter in front of the correct answer.

1. A group of people who make laws and provide services is called
   a. a business.
   b. a government.
   c. a democracy.
   d. a mayor.

2. Rules made by governments are called
   a. voters.
   b. representatives.
   c. laws.
   d. democracy.

3. People who vote for their government live in a
   a. House of Representatives.
   b. democracy.
   c. Congress.
   d. natural resource.

4. The person who leads a state is called the
   a. Senate.
   b. mayor.
   c. President.
   d. governor.

5. Soil, water, and forests are all
   a. climates.
   b. natural resources.
   c. services.
   d. minerals.

6. People who do something to help other people work in
   a. manufacturing.
   b. fishing.
   c. service jobs.
   d. farming.

THINKING AND WRITING

Why is it important for us to protect our natural resources?

_____

_____

_____

_____

_____

_____

_____

Reading a Bar Graph

During the 1800s and early 1900s, most immigrants came from countries in Europe. Use the bar graph below to find out where some of our country's more recent immigrants have come from.

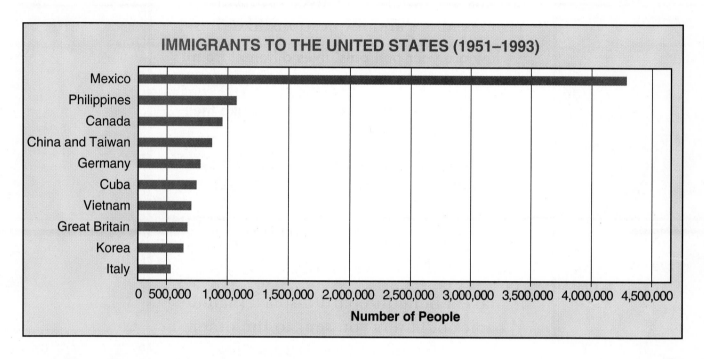

1. What time period does the bar graph cover?

   _____

2. From what country did most immigrants come?

   _____

3. About how many immigrants came from Korea?
   Circle the correct answer.

   500,000   more than 500,000   exactly 1,000,000

4. Compare the bar graph on page 19 to the one on this page. How are they alike? How are they different?

   _____

   _____

Now it's time to finish your unit project. Think about what you learned about your pen pals and where they live. Talk with your classmates about questions like these.

- **How are your pen pals' lives different from yours?**

- **How does the climate they live in make their life different from yours?**

- **How are the natural resources where they live different from those where you live?**

Decide how you want to show the results of your project. Choose one of these ways or use one of your own ideas.

➤ Make a bulletin board display. Include copies of letters you sent to the other class and copies of the letters they wrote to you. Include a map that shows where you live in the United States and where they live.

➤ Work with another group from your class to report to another class about your pen pals. Talk to them about your project. Share your letters with them. Show them on a map where your pen pals live.

The Northeast Region

Let's visit the Northeast Region. This region is made up of 11 states. You may already know something about the Northeast Region. Perhaps you know that New York City is in the Northeast.

Unit 2 of this book will help you answer questions like these about the Northeast Region.

- What is the land like in the Northeast?
- Which city is our nation's capital?
- What kinds of jobs are there in the Northeast?

UNIT PROJECT

Start a team project. Plan a trip to places in the Northeast. Make a travel brochure about the places. Work on the project as you read Unit 2.

Geography of the Northeast Region

You may already know something about the geography of the Northeast Region. You know where this region is in the United States. Its name tells where it is.

States and Cities

There are 11 states in the Northeast Region. Look at the map below. Put your finger on each of the states colored purple.

 Find the state in the Northeast Region that is the farthest north. Write N on that state.

Find the state that is the farthest south. Write S on that state.

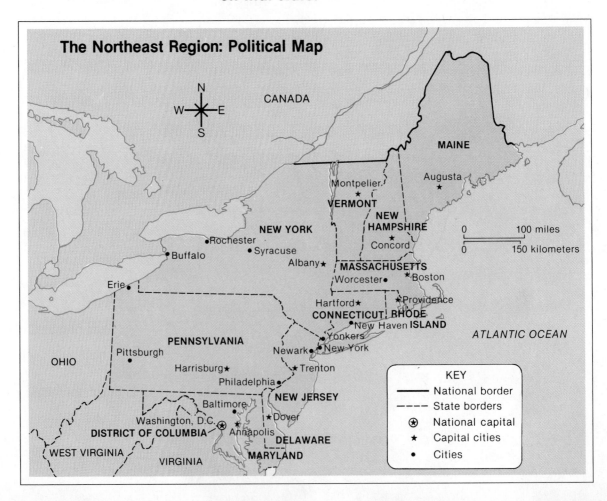

The Northeast Region: Political Map

CANADA

MAINE

Augusta ★

Montpelier ★

VERMONT

NEW HAMPSHIRE

NEW YORK

Concord ★

Rochester ●

● Syracuse

● Buffalo

Albany ★

MASSACHUSETTS

Worcester ● ★ Boston

Erie ●

Hartford ★ ★ Providence

CONNECTICUT RHODE ISLAND

● New Haven

PENNSYLVANIA

● Yonkers

Newark ● ● New York

OHIO

Pittsburgh ●

Harrisburg ★ ★ Trenton

Philadelphia ●

NEW JERSEY

Baltimore ●

Washington, D.C. ⊛ ★ Dover

DISTRICT OF COLUMBIA ★ Annapolis

DELAWARE

WEST VIRGINIA MARYLAND

VIRGINIA

ATLANTIC OCEAN

0   100 miles
0   150 kilometers

KEY
—— National border
----- State borders
⊛ National capital
★ Capital cities
● Cities

This photograph shows three important government buildings in Washington, D.C. The building in the center of the photograph is the United States Capitol. Behind the Capitol and to the left is the Supreme Court Building. The building next to it is the Library of Congress.

A **capital** is a city where a government meets. Washington, D.C., is the capital of our country. It is in the Northeast Region. Washington, D.C., is not like any other city in the United States. It's in a special place called the District of Columbia. We shorten District of Columbia to D.C.

 Find Washington, D.C., on the map on page 34. It's in the southern part of the region. Use the map key. Find the special star for the national capital. Circle the same star on the map.

Every state has a capital, too. The state government meets there. There are 11 state capitals in the Northeast Region.

 The map has a distance scale. You can use it to find out how far places are from each other. Find Washington, D.C., again on the map on page 34. Use the scale. About how far away is Washington from the capital of Pennsylvania?

The Land and Water

Pretend that you are planning a bike trip in the Northeast Region. You're going to start on the coast of Maine. Remember, the coast is where the land is next to the ocean. Look at the map key below. You can see that green stands for plains. Biking is easy on the flat plains along the coast!

There are **highlands** west of the coast. Highlands are hilly areas between flat lands and mountains. Biking will be hard.

 Find the color for highlands in the map key. Draw lines from the key to three highland areas.

On the map there is a color for the mountains. Circle the Appalachian Mountains. (Remember, *Mts.* is short for *Mountains.*) Here biking will really be hard!

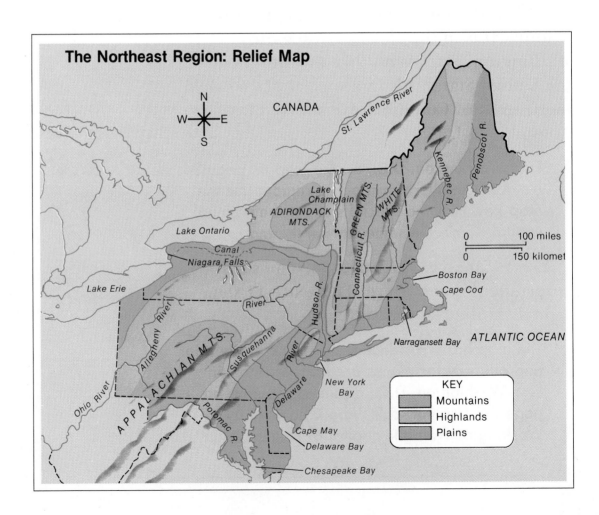

The Northeast Region: Relief Map

New York City is one of the busiest ports in the United States.

You're going to see a lot of water on your trip through the Northeast. Along the coast you will see some large **bays.** A bay is a place where the water is almost surrounded by land. Bays look a little like someone has taken a bite out of the coast.

Bays make safe **harbors** for ships, because the water is protected by land. Some big cities like New York City and Boston are on bays. These cities are **ports.** A port is a place where people can load and unload ships.

Bay

 Look at the map on page 36. Find the names of two bays. Write their names here.

_____

_____

You will cross some big rivers on your trip. The rivers flow into the Atlantic Ocean.

 Look at the map again. Trace two of the rivers that flow into the ocean.

With your team, look at the map on page 36. Do you want to go see mountains or visit the ocean? Collect or draw some pictures of the kind of land you would like to visit.

Eleanor Roosevelt

Eleanor Roosevelt

Eleanor Roosevelt was a famous American who was born in New York City in 1884. Eleanor Roosevelt did a great deal to help make good laws for our country. In the first unit of this book, you learned how we make laws in the United States. You read about Congress and the President. But did you know people like you can help make laws, too?

In 1920 Eleanor Roosevelt began to work to get rights for women. She also helped get laws to protect children. But most of all, she worked to help the poor and the homeless. She wrote articles for newspapers. She gave talks all around the country.

In 1932 Eleanor Roosevelt's husband became President of the United States. He was Franklin Delano Roosevelt. Eleanor Roosevelt told him about the problems she had found with the poor and the homeless.

After her husband died, Eleanor Roosevelt became a representative of the United States in the **United Nations.** The United Nations is a group of many countries of the world that meets in New York City to try to solve problems.

Eleanor Roosevelt has been praised by people around the world. A friend of hers once said no one ever changed so many lives for the better.

What is one reason why Eleanor Roosevelt is famous? Write your answer here.

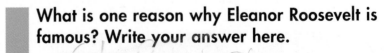

CHAPTER ✓ CHECKUP

Complete each sentence. Circle the letter in front of the correct answer.

1. Two of the states in the Northeast Region are
   a. Virginia and Georgia.
   b. New York and Pennsylvania.
   c. Kansas and Nebraska.
   d. California and Hawaii.

2. A capital is
   a. a place where ships are unloaded.
   b. a city where a government meets.
   c. a large river.
   d. near the ocean.

3. Washington, D.C., is
   a. the capital of the United States.
   b. the capital of Maine.
   c. the capital of New York.
   d. the capital of Washington.

4. The land along the coast of the Northeast is
   a. flat.
   b. hilly.
   c. filled with mountains.
   d. a highland.

5. Places that make safe harbors for ships are
   a. capitals.
   b. highlands.
   c. bays.
   d. mountains.

6. In a port, people
   a. live very close to mountains.
   b. load and unload ships.
   c. work on farms.
   d. get on trains.

THINKING AND WRITING Pretend that you could live any place in the Northeast. Where would you like to live? Why?

_____

_____

_____

_____

_____

_____

_____

People of the Northeast Region

The Northeast Region is not just bays, mountains, and big cities. In this chapter you'll learn about the people of the Northeast. Let's begin by visiting the Northeast in the early 1600s, almost 400 years ago.

Long Ago: The Pilgrims

"Land Ho!" a sailor shouted. The people in the little ship looked through the fog. They saw land! These tired people had left England two months before. They had sailed through many storms. At times, they thought their ship, the *Mayflower*, was going to sink. Now, on November 20, 1620, they had finished their trip across the Atlantic Ocean.

We call these people the Pilgrims. They left England because the laws there allowed only one religion. The Pilgrims wanted to practice their own religion.

So the Pilgrims started a colony in North America. There they built their own church and their own school. They called their new town Plymouth, after the city that had been their home in England.

Why did the Pilgrims leave England? Write your answer here.

forrelig
logs
freedom

The Pilgrims had many problems that first winter. They had little food, and it was too late in the season to plant crops. It was very cold. Almost half the Pilgrims died that winter. The others thought about going back to England.

 How did the climate affect the Pilgrims? Write your answer here.

too cold cohr food

The Pilgrims were saved by the American Indians who lived near Plymouth. American Indians had lived there for thousands of years. They knew how to grow and find food. An American Indian named Squanto taught the Pilgrims how to plant corn, catch fish, and even get maple syrup from trees.

 Why did the American Indians know more about getting food than the Pilgrims? Write your answer here.

They are baties has food.

When spring came, the Pilgrims planted corn and other crops. By the end of the summer, they had a lot of food. They decided to celebrate by having a feast with their new friends.

Before the meal the Pilgrims gave thanks for the good harvest and for the help the American Indians gave them. They gave thanks for being alive in a new land.

This feast was the first Thanksgiving. Many years later, Thanksgiving became a holiday for everyone in the United States.

Where Do People Live in the Northeast Region?

The Pilgrims were some of the first people to move from their country to North America. But over the years, people came to the Northeast from countries around the world. Today more than 57 million people live in the Northeast.

Most people in the Northeast live in cities. Look at the map of the Northeast on page 34. Find Boston, Massachusetts. Then find Washington, D.C. Imagine a straight line between them. If you rode along that line in a car, you would be in cities most of the time.

 Let's see how far away from each other Boston and Washington, D.C., really are. Use the distance scale on the map on page 34. Measure the distance between these two cities. Write the distance here.

_____

Many people in the Northeast live in **suburbs.** Suburbs are towns or small cities near big cities. Many people who live in suburbs work in the city.

People would have to live very close to their jobs if there were no **transportation.** Transportation is the way people travel to places. People drive on highways or take buses or trains.

What kinds of transportation do you use in your community?

_____car_____

_____fix_____

New York City has more people than the states of Maine, Vermont, and New Hampshire added together.

The Charles River runs through the city of Boston. People like to take boats on the river.

You remember that the Pilgrims began a community called Plymouth. Boston, Massachusetts, is a city near Plymouth. Boston was started by other people soon after the Pilgrims came to Plymouth. Look at the picture of Boston above.

Today, Boston is much bigger than Plymouth. One reason Boston is big is because it is by a large bay. Boston is on a river, too. The people who started Boston shipped many goods to England. Boston soon became an important port.

Boston is the capital of Massachusetts. Three other port cities in the Northeast are also state capitals.

Look back at the map on page 34. Can you find the capital cities that are also ports? Write their names here.

_____, Rhode Island

_____, Delaware

_____, Maryland

43

The South East Prospect of The City of Philadelphia By Peter Cooper Painter

(top left) The colonists met in Independence Hall and agreed to make the United States a nation. (top right) This is a painting of the busy harbor in Philadelphia that the colonists used.

One of the most important cities in the region is Baltimore, Maryland. Baltimore is a very old and busy port. Tourists like to visit parts of the old harbor. One area is called Harborplace. People go there to shop and to eat. The National Aquarium is nearby.

Philadelphia, Pennsylvania, is one of the oldest cities in the United States. It was started by William Penn over 300 years ago. Penn's colonists left England so they could practice their own religion.

How are the colonists of Plymouth and Philadelphia alike? Write your answer here.

The both wanted

Look at the picture of Independence Hall on this page. It is in Philadelphia. Over 200 years ago, people from all the colonies met there. On July 4, 1776, they decided to start a new country. Many people visit Independence Hall every year.

UNIT PROJECT Tip Work with your team to find out more about one of the cities in this chapter. List places in that city you would like to visit.

Working in the Northeast Region

The resources of a region create many jobs. Crops need to be harvested. Trees need to be cut and planted. Food needs to be made. One of the most important resources of the Northeast is the Atlantic Ocean.

 There are 11 states in the Northeast. Look at the map on page 34. Count the states that are next to the ocean. Write the answer here.

_____

Can you guess why the Atlantic Ocean is such an important resource? One reason is because it's full of fish!

Early every morning fishing boats leave the ports of the Northeast. They come back with thousands of fish. The fish are sold to stores all over the Northeast and in other regions.

Most people in the Northeast do not work on fishing boats. Many people have service jobs. Remember that service jobs are jobs that help other people. People who work in stores, offices, and restaurants have service jobs. Firefighters, police officers, and teachers are service workers too.

Millions of people watch the news on television each evening.

How does a firefighter help people?

_____

_____

_____

Some service jobs in the Northeast help people in other regions of the country. One of these is television news. Television companies have news offices in the Northeast. These offices get reports from around the world. They show news programs that are seen all over the country.

The Pilgrims had to wait many months for a ship to come with news from England. Today's television news programs can show us things as they happen.

Television is one part of a business that is called the communications business. To **communicate** means to share information. One way people communicate is by talking. Newspapers share news and other information with many people. In fact, any way that news or information goes from one person or place to another is a way of communicating.

Today many people use computers to communicate. Office workers can use computers to send electronic mail, or E-mail, to other workers who are far away. E-mail is a very quick way of communicating information.

Name two ways you communicate.

H̲a̲l̲l̲

F̲I̲X̲

There are many different industries in the Northeast Region. This man works in a shoe factory.

Manufacturing also provides jobs for many people in the Northeast. People manufacture, or make, all kinds of goods. In the Northeast, most of the goods they make are small, like clocks and books. But there are some companies that make airplanes and other big machines.

Clothing is also an important industry in the region. The man in the photograph is putting two parts of a boot together. Someone else made the rubber bottom and another person made the leather part. This man sews the parts together. He can sew a boot in one minute!

If you sailed east on the Atlantic Ocean from Maine, you'd land in Nova Scotia. Nova Scotia is a **province** of Canada. In Canada, provinces are like states in the United States.

Nova Scotia is almost completely surrounded by the Atlantic Ocean. Like the Northeast Region of the United States, the Atlantic Ocean is an important resource for Nova Scotia. People in Nova Scotia catch more fish than any other province in Canada.

Halifax is the capital of Nova Scotia. It is one of the most important ports in Canada. Fish, oil, and steel are just some of the products shipped from the Port of Halifax to the United States and other places.

You might wonder how Nova Scotia got its name. Nova Scotia means "New Scotland." During the 1700s and 1800s, many people from Scotland came to live in Nova Scotia. Certain parts of Nova Scotia look very much like the hilly highlands of Scotland. Some Nova Scotians still celebrate their history with Scottish festivals each year.

A fishing boat docks at a Nova Scotia port.

 Look at the map. Circle the Nova Scotian city nearest the United States.

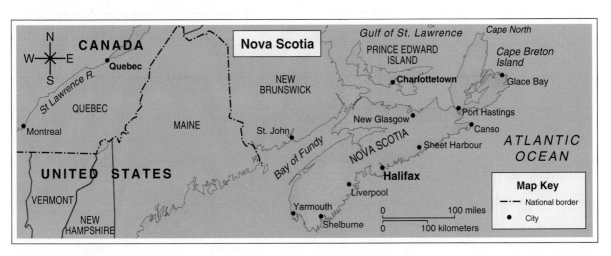

CHAPTER ✓ CHECKUP

Complete each sentence. Circle the letter in front of the correct answer.

1. The Pilgrims came to the Northeast to
   - **a.** learn to plant corn.
   - **b.** be free to practice their religion.
   - **c.** meet American Indians.
   - **d.** find New York.

2. Many people in the Northeast live in
   - **a.** villages.
   - **b.** colonies.
   - **c.** bays.
   - **d.** suburbs.

3. Buses, trains, and cars are types of
   - **a.** communication.
   - **b.** transportation.
   - **c.** manufacturing.
   - **d.** service jobs.

4. Boston and Baltimore are
   - **a.** on the Pacific Ocean.
   - **b.** state capitals.
   - **c.** important port cities.
   - **d.** on the same river.

5. An important resource of the Northeast Region is
   - **a.** the Atlantic Ocean.
   - **b.** television news.
   - **c.** Independence Hall.
   - **d.** clothing.

6. When you communicate you
   - **a.** make goods.
   - **b.** start colonies.
   - **c.** use a computer.
   - **d.** share information.

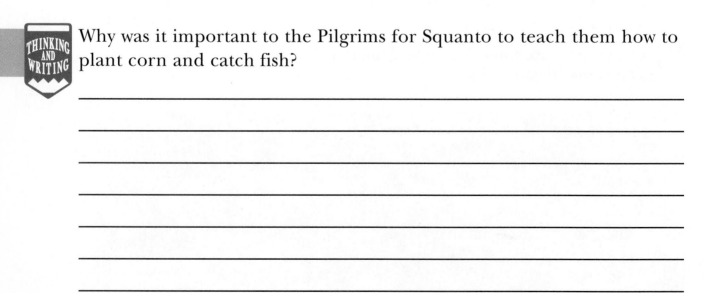

THINKING AND WRITING Why was it important to the Pilgrims for Squanto to teach them how to plant corn and catch fish?

_____

_____

_____

_____

_____

_____

FACTS ABOUT THE STATES OF THE NORTHEAST REGION

STATE Origin of Name *Nickname(s)*	Capital	Population *(estimate)*	Rank	Bird	Flower
Connecticut Mohegan Indian word that means "long tidal river." *Constitution State* *Nutmeg State*	Hartford	3,280,960	**Pop** 27 **Size** 48	Robin	Mountain laurel
Delaware Named for English governor of Virginia. *First State*	Dover	700,000	**Pop** 46 **Size** 49	Blue hen chicken	Peach blossom
Maine May come from sailor's term, *the main*, for the mainland. *Pine Tree State*	Augusta	1,239,000	**Pop** 38 **Size** 39	Chickadee	White pine cone and tassel
Maryland Named for an English queen. *Old Line State* *Free State*	Annapolis	4,965,000	**Pop** 19 **Size** 42	Baltimore oriole	Black-eyed Susan
Massachusetts Algonquian Indian word, means "near the great hill." *Bay State*	Boston	6,012,000	**Pop**. 13 **Size** 45	Chickadee	Mayflower
New Hampshire Named after a county in England. *Granite State*	Concord	1,125,000	**Pop**. 41 **Size** 44	Purple finch	Purple lilac

STATE Origin of Name *Nickname(s)*	Capital	Population *(estimate)*	Rank	Bird	Flower
New Jersey Named for an island in the English Channel. *Garden State*	Trenton	7,879,000	**Pop.** 9 **Size** 46	Eastern goldfinch	Purple violet
New York Named to honor the Duke of York who became the King of England. *Empire State*	Albany	18,197,000	**Pop.** 2 **Size** 30	Bluebird	Rose
Pennsylvania *Penn* for William Penn. *Sylvania* means "woodland." *Keystone State*	Harrisburg	12,048,000	**Pop.** 5 **Size** 33	Ruffed grouse	Mountain laurel
Rhode Island Named for an island in the Mediterranean Sea. *Little Rhody* *The Ocean State*	Providence	1,000,000	**Pop.** 43 **Size** 50	Rhode Island red	Violet
Vermont Name comes from French words for "green mountain." *Green Mountain State*	Montpelier	576,000	**Pop.** 48 **Size** 43	Hermit thrush	Red clover
District of Columbia Honors Christopher Columbus.		606,900		Wood thrush	American Beauty rose

Unit 2 Skill Builder
Using a Distance Scale

In this unit you learned about Washington, D.C., the capital of the United States. Suppose you visited Washington. You would probably want to visit some of the city's famous places. Use the map and the distance scale to find out the distances between some of the places you could visit.

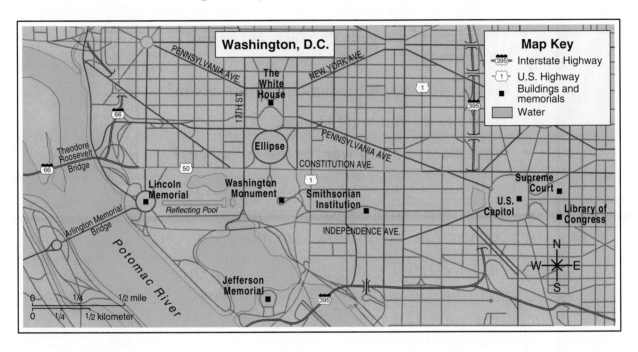

1. Find the White House on the map. Then find the Capitol. How far away is the White House from the Capitol?

_____

2. Suppose that after you visited the Capitol, you visited the Library of Congress. About what distance would you travel?

_____

3. How far away from each other are the Library of Congress and the Lincoln Memorial?

_____

4. The Washington Monument and the Smithsonian Institution look close to each other on the map. What is the real distance between them?

_____

Now it's time to finish your unit project. Think about places you want to visit in the Northeast. Talk with your team about questions like these.

- **What time of the year do you want to visit the Northeast?**

- **Do you want to visit mountains or the ocean?**

- **What city do you want to visit?**

- **What places do you want to see in that city?**

Decide how you want to show the results of your group's project. Choose one of these ways or use one of your own ideas.

➤ Put together a travel brochure. Use the pictures you collected or drew in your brochure. List the places you want to visit and describe the places in your brochure. Display your brochure in the classroom.

➤ Make your travel brochure. Have each group member show a favorite page of the brochure to another team. Tell the other team about the place shown on the page.

➤ Draw a route of your trip on a map. Include the names of cities and other places you will visit. Tell why you planned your route the way you did. Tell how far apart two of the places are.

UNIT 3

The Southeast Region

Now we're going to visit the Southeast Region. The region is made up of 12 states. What do you already know about the Southeast? Maybe you know that the Southeast has lots of warm, sandy beaches—even during the winter!

This unit will help you answer questions like these about the Southeast.

- Why is the Mississippi River important to the Southeast?

- What was life like in a town in the Southeast long ago?

- What kinds of jobs are there in the Southeast?

UNIT PROJECT

Start a team project. Imagine your team is traveling through the Southeast Region on the Mississippi River. Explain in journal entries what you might see as you travel down the river. Work on your project as you read Unit 3.

Geography of the Southeast Region

Welcome to the Southeast Region! It's a land of long, hot summers and mild winters. It's a land of wide plains, rolling hills, and tall mountains.

Where Is the Southeast Region?

There are 12 states in the Southeast Region. Put your finger on each of the dark green states on the map below.

 **Write an <u>S</u> on the state that is farthest south.
Write an <u>N</u> on the state that is farthest north.**

The Southeast Region: Political Map

KEY
- - - - State borders
★ Capital cities
• Cities

0   100 miles
0   200 kilometers

Like the states of the Northeast Region, many states in the Southeast Region are next to the Atlantic Ocean.

 Look at the map on page 54. Find the states that are next to the Atlantic Ocean. Circle the names of those states.

The southern part of the Southeast Region is near the Gulf of Mexico. Like a bay, a **gulf** is a large body of water that joins an ocean. It is partly surrounded by land. Find the Gulf of Mexico on the map.

Certain kinds of bad weather begin over large bodies of water. A **hurricane** is a storm with very strong winds and heavy rain. Some hurricanes start over the Gulf of Mexico and the Atlantic Ocean. Some hit the coast of the Southeast. Hurricanes can kill people. They can destroy buildings and crops.

Look at this table about hurricanes. A table lists facts so you can compare them easily. Which hurricane caused the most damage? Write the name of the hurricane and the year here.

Andrew

Hurricanes of the Southeast			
Name of Hurricane	Year	States Hardest Hit by Hurricane	Cost of Damage
Andrew	1992	Florida, Louisiana	$7,250,000,000
Hugo	1989	South Carolina	$7,000,000,000
Frederic	1979	Alabama, Mississippi	$2,250,000,000
Camille	1969	Mississippi, Louisiana, Alabama	$1,500,000,000

Plain

What Is the Land Like?

If you took a bike trip in the Southeast, you would have lots of flat plains to ride on. The plains near the Atlantic Ocean are called the Coastal Plain because they are near the coast. They have good soil and lots of water.

 Put your pencil on the plains at the upper right part of this map. Trace a bike route as far south as you can. Make an <u>X</u> where you stop.

Find the Savannah River. Suppose you decide to ride northwest along the river. Look at the map key. Would riding your bike get harder or easier? Why?

Missppi River

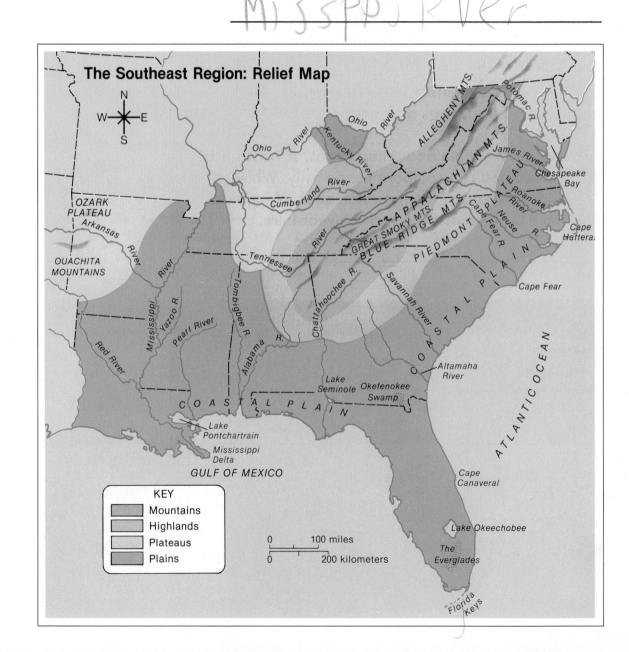

The Southeast Region: Relief Map

N W E S

Ohio River
Ohio River
Kentucky River
Ohio River
ALLEGHENY MTS.
Potomac R.
James River
Chesapeake Bay
Cumberland River
APPALACHIAN MTS.
Roanoke River
OZARK PLATEAU
Arkansas River
GREAT SMOKY MTS.
BLUE RIDGE MTS.
PLATEAU
Cape Fear R.
Neuse R.
OUACHITA MOUNTAINS
Tennessee River
PIEDMONT
Cape Hatteras
Mississippi River
Yazoo R.
Tombigbee R.
Chattahoochee R.
Savannah River
COASTAL PLAIN
Cape Fear
Pearl River
Alabama R.
Altamaha River
Red River
Lake Seminole
Okefenokee Swamp
ATLANTIC OCEAN
C O A S T A L   P L A I N
Lake Pontchartrain
Mississippi Delta
GULF OF MEXICO
Cape Canaveral
Lake Okeechobee
The Everglades
Florida Keys

KEY
Mountains
Highlands
Plateaus
Plains

0   100 miles
0   200 kilometers

There are **swamps** in some parts of the Coastal Plain. A swamp is a place where the land is always wet. The <u>X</u> you made on the map on page 56 is near the Everglades swamp. Many plants and animals live in swamps. Alligators are one kind of animal that lives in the Everglades.

Look at the map and map key on page 56. Find the mountains. They are called the Appalachian Mountains.

 Now look at the western part of the map. What is the longest river you see? Write your answer here.

_____

The Mississippi River runs through the western plains of the region. It is the second longest river in the United States. This river begins far north, in Minnesota. It travels south 2,340 miles to the Gulf of Mexico. The Mississippi is so wide that big ships can travel on it. The ships carry oil, coal, cotton, and many other products.

The Mississippi River is so full of soil that it looks like mud. Rains add water to the river. When the river has too much water in it, some spills out onto the land. Water that rises and covers the land is called a **flood.**

Floods can hurt people and damage their homes. But Mississippi floods also do some good. They leave **fertile** soil on fields. Fertile soil is land that is good for growing crops.

(top) Trees, vines, and flowers grow on the wet land of a swamp.
(bottom) These barges are carrying coal on the Mississippi River near New Orleans.

 **UNIT PROJECT Tip** With your team, find out what the ships and boats on the Mississippi look like. Draw pictures of the ships in your journal. Write about the products the ships carry.

China

Do you eat much rice? Most Americans eat about eight pounds of rice every year. But in China, rice is the main food. The average Chinese person eats more than 200 pounds of rice each year!

China is the largest rice-growing country in the world. China has many areas of flat, wet land that are perfect for growing rice. In China, farmers plant small rice plants by hand. It takes many workers to plant the rice. They also harvest, or pick, the rice by hand.

One of the biggest food crops of Arkansas, Louisiana, and Mississippi is rice. Farmers in these states use big machines to plant and harvest rice. Because of the machines, fewer people are needed to plant and harvest rice in the United States than in China.

Why do you think farmers plant rice in the Southeast? Write your answer here.

_____

Chinese farmers are planting young rice plants in the flooded fields.

CHAPTER ✓ CHECKUP

Complete each sentence. Circle the letter in front of the correct answer.

1. A gulf is like

  a. a bay.

  b. a river.

  c. a lake.

  d. an ocean.

2. Hurricanes begin over the Gulf of Mexico or over the

  a. Mississippi River.

  b. Southeast.

  c. Northeast.

  d. Atlantic Ocean.

3. The Coastal Plain is flat and has lots of

  a. mountains.

  b. hurricanes.

  c. good soil.

  d. snow.

4. A swamp is

  a. dry.

  b. wet.

  c. snowy.

  d. very hot.

5. The second longest river in the United States is the

  a. Everglades.

  b. Savannah.

  c. Mississippi.

  d. Ohio.

6. Water that rises and covers the land is a

  a. hurricane.

  b. gulf.

  c. swamp.

  d. flood.

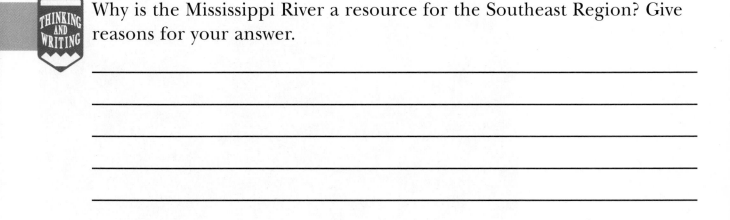

THINKING AND WRITING Why is the Mississippi River a resource for the Southeast Region? Give reasons for your answer.

_____

_____

_____

_____

_____

_____

_____

CHAPTER 7

People of the Southeast Region

What is it like to live in the Southeast Region? Let's find out! First, we'll visit the region 200 years ago.

Long Ago: Old Virginia in 1774

It's two o'clock and time for lunch. The King's Arms Tavern in Williamsburg, Virginia, is filled with people today.

The government of the colony meets here. Representatives from Virginia come to Williamsburg, the capital, to discuss laws.

 Today, Williamsburg is not the capital of Virginia. Look at the map on page 54 and find the capital of Virginia. Write the name here.

_____

Many people stay in taverns, or hotels, like the King's Arms. People still visit the King's Arms Tavern today.

The first governor wanted Williamsburg to become a big city. He made the streets straight, not like the curving streets in country towns. The main street of this city is 100 feet wide!

Williamsburg has a school but not everyone can go there. Most children have to help their parents in their shops. Slaves are not allowed to go to school. But there is a school for American Indians who want to learn to read and write English.

Williamsburg has lots of stores. Do you need a new pair of shoes? You can't just walk into a shoe store and buy them. First, the shoemaker has to measure your feet. Then he'll make shoes to fit you. You can come back in a week to pick them up.

There are many businesses here in Williamsburg. There's a blacksmith who works with iron and steel. He makes shoes for horses and fixes tools. And there are shops where barrels or baskets or wigs are made. People in Williamsburg wear wigs whenever they get dressed up.

That's how it was in 1774. If you visit Williamsburg today, you'll have a surprise. It never became a big city. In fact, it still looks the same! The King's Arms still serves meals, and people still make baskets by hand. That is because the city is a "living museum" where we can go to see how Americans lived here more than 200 years ago.

This man weaves a basket in Williamsburg today. He is dressed in colonial clothing.

Write the name of a building in your town that you think should always be kept the way it is now. Tell why.

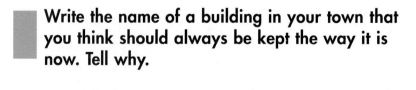

These children are enjoying one of the beaches in the Southeast Region.

Who Lives in the Southeast Today?

More than 61 million people live in the Southeast. Almost as many people live in the Northeast. But the Southeast is not as crowded.

 Compare the maps on page 34 and page 54. Which region has more land?

Every year, more people move to the Southeast. Some people come to find jobs. Others come because they like warm weather. The lower part of the region is called the **Sunbelt** because it has lots of sun.

People have moved to the Southeast from many parts of the world. From the 1600s to the early 1900s, many people came from Europe. Since the 1960s, thousands of people from Cuba have moved to Florida. People from China, the Philippines, and Vietnam have come to the region, too. Almost half of all African Americans in the United States live in the Southeast.

Many older people who have completed their careers move to the Southeast Region.

Where Do People Live in the Region?

In the Southeast, more people live in small towns than in cities. But there are large cities in each state of the region. New Orleans, Louisiana, is the busiest port city in the United States. It is on the Mississippi River.

Products and crops from many states are shipped to New Orleans on the river. At New Orleans they are put on bigger ships. From the Mississippi River, the ships move out into the Gulf of Mexico. From the Gulf of Mexico, they can go around the world.

 Look at the map on page 56. Ships leave the Gulf of Mexico to take products to other countries. If they go east, on what ocean will they travel?

Lacy iron railings decorate many buildings in the part of New Orleans known as the French Quarter.

New Orleans was once a colony of France. Later, France sold New Orleans to the United States. Some of the buildings in New Orleans look like old buildings in France. Other parts look very modern. The big round building in the photograph is the Superdome. Inside the Superdome there is a football field.

The Superdome in New Orleans can hold more than 95,000 people.

The warm climate of the Southeast is good for growing certain crops. Most of the oranges grown in our country come from Florida. Another important crop of the Southeast is peanuts. Did you know that peanut soup and peanut pie are popular foods in parts of the Southeast?

One city in the Southeast is known for a very different kind of product. Nashville, Tennessee, is called the capital of country music. Stars of country music make records there. The music business is one of the biggest businesses in the city.

Many people in the Southeast have service jobs. People all over the Southeast work in hotels, restaurants, stores, movie theaters, and in many other places where they help other people.

List three important crops of the Southeast. Write your answer here.

(top) An orange grove in Florida
(right) The Grand Old Opry is a famous part of Nashville's history with country music.

UNIT
PROJECT
Tip

There are many cotton farms along the Mississippi River. Find out what other crops people grow along the Mississippi River. Write an entry in your journal about one of the crops.

Sometimes people do simple things that change everyone's life. Rosa Parks changed our lives one day when she sat down in a bus.

In 1955 Rosa Parks lived in Montgomery, Alabama. At that time there were many laws in the Southeast that were not fair to African Americans. These laws said that African Americans could sit only in the back part of buses. They also said that African Americans had to give up their seat if a white person wanted to sit down.

One afternoon Rosa Parks sat down on a bus. She had worked hard that day and was tired. A white man asked her to move so he could sit down. Mrs. Parks refused. The police came and arrested her.

Rosa Parks

What was unfair about the laws in Montgomery? Write your answer here.

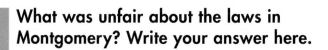

_____

_____

When African Americans in Montgomery heard what happened, they became angry. Everyone paid the same amount to get on the bus. Why couldn't they all sit where they wanted to sit?

African Americans decided not to use the city buses until the laws were changed. For more than a year, they didn't ride city buses. The city bus company lost a lot of money. Finally, the city changed the law.

After that, African Americans in the Southeast began trying to change other laws that were not fair. Today those laws are gone.

Complete each sentence. Circle the letter in front of the correct answer.

1. The city that still looks the way it did about 200 years ago is
   a. Atlanta.
   b. New Orleans.
   c. Miami.
   d. Williamsburg.

2. The Mississippi River is important to the city of New Orleans because
   a. the city needs a lot of water.
   b. ships carry products on it.
   c. farmers like to swim in the river.
   d. it is next to the Superdome.

3. The busiest port city in the United States is
   a. New Orleans.
   b. Miami.
   c. Atlanta.
   d. Williamsburg.

4. Atlanta became a big city after
   a. the Superdome was built.
   b. the farmers left.
   c. railroads reached the city.
   d. plantations were started.

5. Long ago, the biggest crop in the Southeast was
   a. cotton.
   b. peanuts.
   c. oranges.
   d. rice.

6. The city of Nashville is known for its
   a. buildings.
   b. music.
   c. railroads.
   d. blue jeans.

 THINKING AND WRITING

Would you like to visit a place that still looks the way it did 200 years ago? Give your reasons.

_____

_____

_____

_____

_____

FACTS ABOUT THE STATES
OF THE SOUTHEAST REGION

STATE Origin of Name *Nickname(s)*	Capital	Population *(estimate)*	Rank	Bird	Flower
Alabama Named for Choctaw Indians. Word may mean "I clear the thicket." *Yellowhammer State* *Heart of Dixie*	Montgomery	4,218,792	**Pop.** 22 **Size** 30	Common flicker	Camellia
Arkansas Indian word meaning "downstream people." *Land of Opportunity*	Little Rock	2,452,000	**Pop.** 33 **Size** 29	Mockingbird	Apple blossom
Florida Named by Ponce de Leon. Word means "full of flowers" in Spanish. *Sunshine State*	Tallahassee	13,952,714	**Pop.** 4 **Size** 22	Mockingbird	Orange blossom
Georgia Named for an English king. *Empire State of the South* *Peach State*	Atlanta	7,055,336	**Pop.** 11 **Size** 24	Brown thrasher	Cherokee rose
Kentucky Indian word that may mean "meadow-land" or "land of tomorrow." *Bluegrass State*	Frankfort	3,826,794	**Pop.** 24 **Size** 37	Kentucky Cardinal	Goldenrod
Louisiana Named for a French king. *Pelican State* *Bayou State*	Baton Rouge	4,315,085	**Pop.** 21 **Size** 31	Brown pelican	Magnolia

STATE Origin of Name *Nickname(s)*	Capital	Population *(estimate)*	Rank	Bird	Flower
Mississippi Indian word that means "father of waters." *Magnolia State*	Jackson	2,669,111	**Pop.** 31 **Size** 32	Mockingbird	Magnolia
North Carolina Named for an English king. *Tar Heel State*	Raleigh	7,069,836	**Pop.** 10 **Size** 28	Cardinal	Dogwood
South Carolina Named for an English king. *Palmetto State*	Columbia	3,663,984	**Pop.** 25 **Size** 40	Carolina wren	Carolina yellow jessamine
Tennessee Name for a Cherokee Indian village. *Volunteer State* *Big Bend State*	Nashville	5,175,240	**Pop.** 17 **Size** 36	Mockingbird	Iris
Virginia Named for an English queen. *Old Dominion* *Mother of Presidents*	Richmond	6,551,522	**Pop.** 12 **Size** 35	Cardinal	Dogwood
West Virginia Named for an English queen. *Mountain State*	Charleston	1,822,021	**Pop.** 35 **Size** 41	Cardinal	Rhododendron

Unit 3 Skill Builder

Reading a Table

You have read about some famous places in the Southeast Region. The table below tells you about more interesting places. Maybe you've already heard of some of them!

Famous Places in the Southeast Region		
Place	**Location**	**Description**
Mammoth Cave	Kentucky	Unusual cave containing lakes, rivers, and waterfalls
Okefenokee Swamp	Georgia	Large swamp that is home to raccoons, opossums, alligators, bobcats, and many types of birds and plants
Walt Disney World	Florida	Huge amusement park visited by millions of people from around the world

Use the table to answer these questions.

1. What state would you be in if you were visiting Okefenokee Swamp?

____

2. If you visited Kentucky, what famous place could you visit?

____

3. Which famous place would you visit if you wanted to see interesting animals?

____

4. Which place was built by people?

____

Now it's time to finish your unit project. Think about what you learned about the Mississippi River. Talk with your team about questions like these.

- **Why is the Mississippi River important to the Southeast Region?**

- **What states does the Mississippi River pass through?**

- **How do businesses use the Mississippi River?**

- **What crops grow near the Mississippi?**

Decide how you want to show the results of your project. Choose one of these ways or use one of your own ideas.

➤ Make a travel journal to share with other groups in your class. Use a computer to publish your team's journal. If possible, scan photos and your ship artwork into your journal. Pass out copies of your published journal to other classes.

➤ Place your team's journal entries and artwork in a folder. Give your journal a title. Illustrate the cover of the folder.

➤ Read your team's journal entries aloud to the class. Take turns with your team members reading the entries. Use your voice and the pictures you drew to bring the trip to life.

UNIT 4

The North Central Region

Now we're going to go north again. We'll go west, too. We are headed for the North Central Region. The North Central Region is made up of 12 states. Do you know something about the region already? Maybe you know that the North Central Region is where most American cars are built.

In this unit you will find answers to questions like these about the North Central Region.

- What does the land look like?
- What was life like long ago on the plains of this region?
- What kinds of jobs are there in the North Central Region?

UNIT PROJECT

Start a team project. Plan a trip to a city in the North Central Region. Find out how you could get to the city from where you live. Draw up a plan of things to do in that city. Work on your project as you read Unit 4.

73

Geography of the North Central Region

Like the Southeast Region, the North Central Region has 12 states. But the North Central Region is much flatter than the Southeast. There are few mountains and hills.

States, Cities, and Transportation

 Pretend you have to drive to the 12 state capitals in the region. You can go into each state only once. Start in Columbus, Ohio. Use a pencil to draw lines to connect the 12 capitals on the map below.

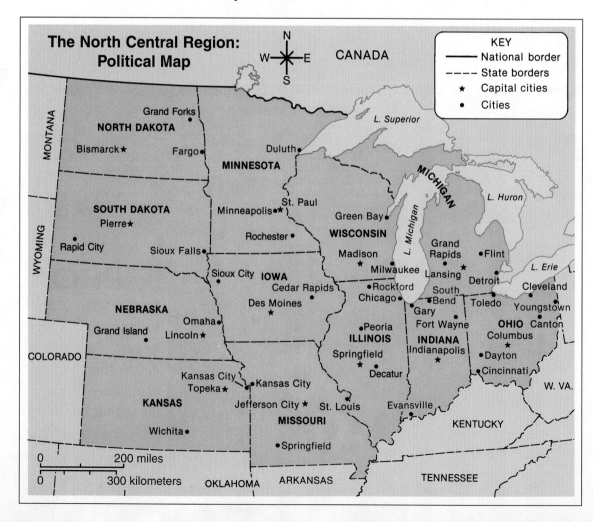

The North Central Region: Political Map

KEY
— National border
---- State borders
★ Capital cities
• Cities

CANADA

L. Superior

MONTANA

Grand Forks
NORTH DAKOTA
Bismarck ★   Fargo •

Duluth •

MINNESOTA

MICHIGAN

L. Huron

SOUTH DAKOTA
Pierre ★

Minneapolis • ★ St. Paul

Green Bay •

WISCONSIN

Grand Rapids •

• Flint

L. Michigan

WYOMING

Rapid City •

Sioux Falls •

Rochester •

Madison ★

Milwaukee •

Lansing ★

L. Erie

Detroit •

Cleveland •

Sioux City •

IOWA

Cedar Rapids •

• Rockford

South Bend •

Toledo •

Youngstown •

NEBRASKA

Des Moines ★

Chicago •

Gary •

Fort Wayne •

OHIO   Canton •

Omaha •

• Peoria

INDIANA

Columbus ★

Grand Island •

Lincoln ★

ILLINOIS

Springfield ★

Indianapolis ★

• Dayton

COLORADO

Decatur •

Cincinnati •

Kansas City •
Topeka ★   • Kansas City

W. VA.

KANSAS

Jefferson City ★   St. Louis •

Evansville •

MISSOURI

KENTUCKY

Wichita •

0   200 miles

0   300 kilometers

• Springfield

OKLAHOMA   ARKANSAS

TENNESSEE

The lines you drew on page 74 show a **route** of travel. A route is the way to go someplace. Look at the four maps on this page. Each map shows a different kind of transportation route. Airplanes fly between cities. Ships go on lakes and rivers. Cars and trucks drive on highways. Trains travel on railroads.

 Look at the map called Main Air Routes. Each green line shows an airplane route. Which city has the most airplanes flying in and out of it? Write your answer here.

_____

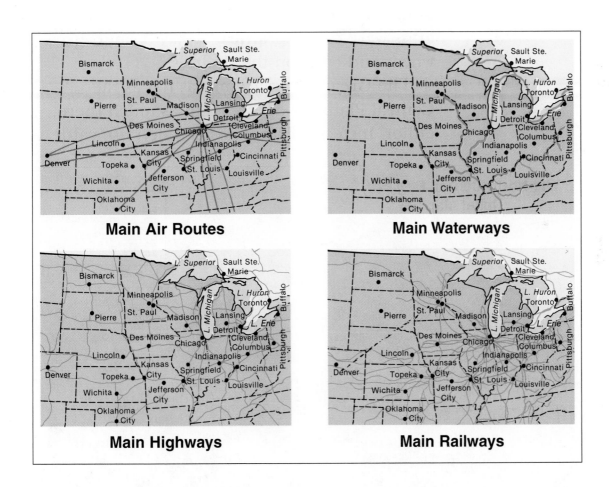

Main Air Routes

Main Waterways

Main Highways

Main Railways

 Find out how far the city your team chose is from where you live. Use the four route maps on this page to choose a route to take to the city.

Prairie

The Land and the Great Lakes

When you studied relief maps of other regions, you learned that the key shows the colors that stand for different landforms.

 Look at the map and the key. Write the name of the landform that makes up most of the North Central Region.

_____

Look at the west side of the map. Circle the words _Great Plains_ and _Central Plains._

The Central Plains are very flat. They were once covered with grass. In some places the grass was nine feet tall! These great areas of grass were called **prairies.** Today farmers grow wheat and corn on the prairies.

The Great Plains are not as flat as the Central Plains. It doesn't rain as much there, either. Instead of farming, people raise cattle.

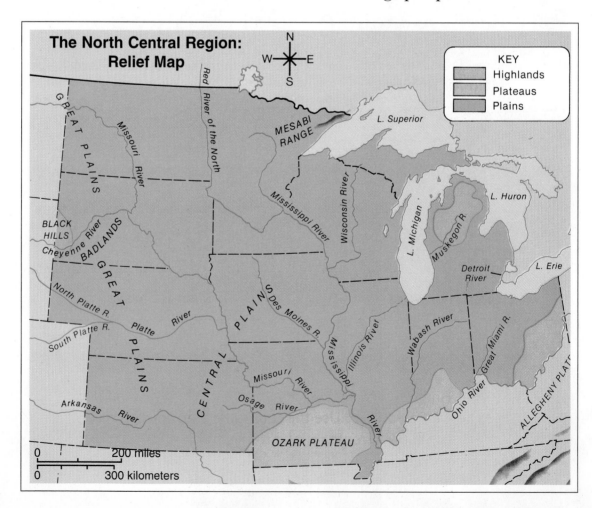

The North Central Region: Relief Map

KEY
Highlands
Plateaus
Plains

GREAT PLAINS
Missouri River
Red River of the North
MESABI RANGE
L. Superior
Wisconsin River
Mississippi River
L. Huron
BLACK HILLS
Cheyenne River
BADLANDS
GREAT
L. Michigan
Muskegon R.
Detroit River
L. Erie
North Platte R.
South Platte R.
Platte River
PLAINS
CENTRAL
Des Moines R.
Illinois River
Wabash River
Great Miami R.
Ohio River
ALLEGHENY PLAT.
PLAINS
Missouri River
Mississippi River
Arkansas River
Osage River
OZARK PLATEAU

0   200 miles
0   300 kilometers

The North Central Region has lakes and rivers that ships can travel on. Some cities in the North Central Region are important ports.

 Find the four biggest lakes on the map on page 76. Write their names here.

_____

_____

We call these large lakes the Great Lakes. There is a fifth Great Lake, called Lake Ontario. It is in the Northeast Region. You can see Lake Ontario on the map on page 36.

Turn back to page 75. Look at the Main Waterways map. You can see that short rivers connect the Great Lakes. Longer rivers connect these lakes to cities and other rivers.

Look at the map on page 76. Find the dotted blue line that leads from Lake Michigan to the Illinois River. The dotted line is a **canal.** A canal is a waterway built by people. Canals link bodies of water so ships can travel from one waterway to another.

 On the map on page 76, trace with a pencil the route a ship would take from Lake Michigan to the Mississippi River.

The Soo Canal and locks are between Lakes Superior and Huron.

Hamburg

Hamburg is a city in the north of Germany, a country across the Atlantic Ocean. Hamburg is a manufacturing and transportation center, just like some of the cities of the North Central Region.

Hamburg has many kinds of factories. Some of the goods manufactured in Hamburg include steel, machines, food products, and even ships!

One of the most important places in Hamburg is the harbor. The harbor is known as "the gateway to the world." More than 15,000 ships from 100 countries use Hamburg's harbor. Ships from all over the world bring fruit, oil, paper, and other products to Hamburg. There are railroads near the harbor that take manufactured products to and from the ships and other cities.

 How is Hamburg like some of the cities in the North Central Region?

_____

Hamburg, Germany, is an important port city.

78

Read each question. Circle the letter in front of the correct answer.

1. What is most of the land like in the North Central Region?

    a. hilly

    b. mostly rivers

    c. flat

    d. mostly plateaus

2. Which city has a very busy airport?

    a. Duluth

    b. Kansas City

    c. St. Louis

    d. Chicago

3. The two areas of plains in the North Central Region are the Great Plains and the

    a. Prairie Plains.

    b. Central Plains.

    c. Middle Plains.

    d. Northern Plains.

4. What is a prairie?

    a. a small mountain

    b. a great area of grass

    c. a large farm

    d. a lake

5. A waterway built by people is a

    a. canal.

    b. route.

    c. harbor.

    d. Great Lake.

6. Which of these is *not* a Great Lake?

    a. Superior

    b. Huron

    c. Minnesota

    d. Erie

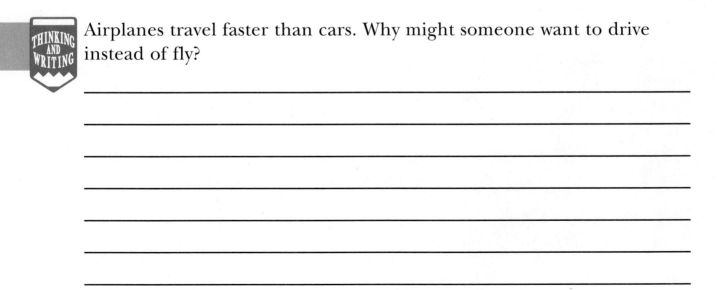

THINKING AND WRITING Airplanes travel faster than cars. Why might someone want to drive instead of fly?

_____

_____

_____

_____

_____

_____

_____

People of the North Central Region

Many people went to the plains of the North Central Region in the 1800s. They were **pioneers**—people who go to live in a new place. Let's read a letter written in 1886 from Molly to her Cousin Barbara. Molly writes about the trip her pioneer family took to the Great Plains.

Long Ago: The Treeless Plains

September 2, 1886
Dear Cousin Barbara,

You wanted to know how we are getting along since leaving Indiana. Well, I will tell you.

Two years ago, my mother and father decided to go to Nebraska where there was a lot of free land. The government said anyone who would build a farm could have the land. This is called **homesteading.** My parents thought that sounded like a pretty good deal.

We left Indiana in a covered wagon. There is a railroad to Omaha, Nebraska, but tickets cost a lot of money. And my parents had to take along all their farm tools. We knew there weren't many stores in Nebraska.

Write the names of some things you think Molly's pioneer family needed.

_____

_____

_____

We were very happy when we left for Nebraska. We sang songs all the way to the Mississippi River. There we met a man who said, "You're headed for the Great American Desert? Well, good luck, you'll need it."

He didn't mean the kind of desert that's full of sand. He meant that the land was flat and empty. Here in Nebraska there are no trees at all, just tall grass. And there aren't many rivers.

 What landform is Molly talking about? Write your answer here.

_____

When we reached our land in Nebraska, Father grabbed a shovel and started digging.

"Look at this color," Father said. "This is the richest dirt I've ever seen. It will be easy to grow crops here."

Since there are no trees, my parents could not build the usual kind of house. Instead, they made one out of **sod.** Sod is blocks of dirt with grass growing in it. The roots of the grass hold the dirt together. My parents piled the blocks of sod on top of one another. Finally, we got our one-room sod house built.

It is dark inside our sod house. But it stays cool in the hot summers and warm in the cold winters.

I hope you and your family are well. Telling you about our life here in Nebraska has been fun. I hope you'll write again soon.

Love,
Cousin Molly

■ **Look at the pictures on pages 80 and 81. The pioneers are plowing fields and making butter. How do people do these things today?**

_____

How Many People Live in the Region Today?

Over 58 million people live in the 12 states of the North Central Region. But more than half of these people live in just three states: Illinois, Ohio, and Michigan.

Why don't more people live in the other nine states? The main reason is that the nine states are where the farms are. Farms need lots of space.

Population is the number of people who live in a place. A population map gives you an idea of how many people live in an area. It also shows you where people live.

Look at the map of Nebraska. The red dots show where people live in that state. Notice that the dots are very far apart in some areas of the state. Those are farm areas. Now look at the map of Ohio. Most of the dots are near cities.

Many people in Chicago take "the el," or elevated train, to work.

 Circle the state that has more people.

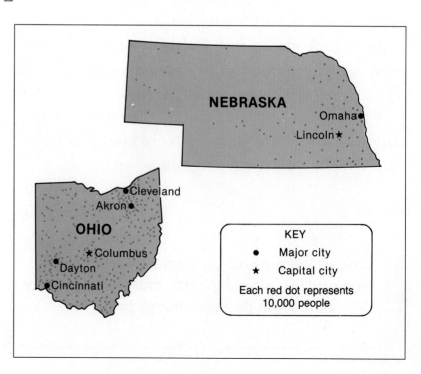

Where Do People Live in the Region?

You know that most people in the region live in Illinois, Ohio, and Michigan. All of these states are near the Great Lakes. Many of the large cities of the region are ports on the Great Lakes. That's because there are many factories and businesses there. Let's take a look at some of these cities.

Chicago, Illinois, is the largest city in the region. It is the third largest city in the United States. Almost three million people live there. Since the 1960s many immigrants from Mexico and Asia have moved to Chicago.

 Find Chicago on the map on page 74. What Great Lake is it next to? Write your answer here.

Chicago is a major transportation center. It is a major port. O'Hare Airport in Chicago is one of the largest and busiest airports in the world. Chicago is also a major center for railroad transportation.

(above) The Michigan Avenue bridge is one of many over the Chicago River that runs through downtown Chicago. (below) This is an exhibit at the DuSable Museum of African-American History. The museum is named after Chicago's first known settler, Jean Baptiste Point du Sable.

More than 80,000 people live in Duluth, Minnesota. Duluth is an important port city. Products like iron ore and grain are sent from Duluth to other places in huge ships. Some ships are as long as four city blocks!

 One place the iron ore is shipped to is Gary, Indiana. Find Duluth and Gary on the map on page 74. What lakes would a ship travel across to get from Duluth to Gary? Draw the route you would follow on the map on page 74.

St. Louis, Missouri, is a port on the Mississippi River. It began as a French colony. American Indians and other people took furs there to sell. People traveling west found it easy to get to St. Louis. Soon the city became a major port and a railroad center.

Today, all kinds of products are shipped from St. Louis. It is a bigger port than Chicago.

So many pioneers passed through St. Louis, Missouri, that it was called "the gateway to the west." The Gateway Arch celebrates that fact.

 Find out about some of the interesting places in the city your team chose. Make a list of those places and write a description for each.

Working in the North Central Region

Service businesses are very important in the North Central Region. Other businesses are also important to the region. Near the Great Lakes, people manufacture a lot of things. On the plains, people have farms and ranches.

Most American cars are made near the Great Lakes. Detroit, Michigan, is the center of the automobile business. In 1903, Henry Ford built a factory in Detroit and began making cars. His "Model T" was the first automobile that many people could buy.

The Model T was made on an **assembly line.** Each worker does one job over and over again on the cars on the assembly line.

Would you like to work on an assembly line? Why? Write your answer here.

_____

_____

Cars are still built on an assembly line.

One of the reasons Henry Ford decided to build his factory in Detroit was because it is a port. Detroit is on a river between Lake Huron and Lake Erie. Ships carrying steel and other things used to build cars arrive in Detroit every day. Other ships carry finished cars from Detroit to other cities and to countries around the world.

Ships also travel across the Great Lakes carrying grains such as corn and wheat and other foods. Corn is the biggest crop grown in the North Central Region. Corn farmers of the region grow more corn than any other farmers in the world.

A lot of the grain grown in the region is fed to cattle and other animals. That's because there are many farms in the North Central Region that just raise animals.

 What kind of land do a lot of ranchers use to raise animals in the region?

Dairy cattle are raised in every state of the region. We get milk, cheese, and other foods from dairy cattle. Part of your breakfast this morning may have come from a cow in Iowa!

(above) This Great Lakes freighter unloads cargo at Hancock, Michigan. (below) Machinery helps today's farmers not only milk their cows but also keep track of all milk production.

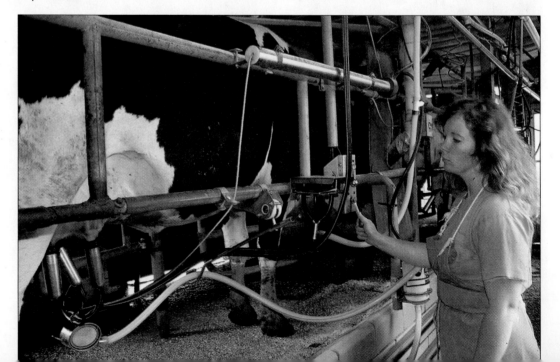

Special People

Abraham Lincoln was the first President from the North Central Region. He was born in Kentucky in 1809. When he was seven, his family moved to Indiana. Abe and his father cut down trees and built a house and furniture for the Lincoln family.

 What resource did the Lincolns use to make their house? Write you answer here.

_____

Young Abe spent less than a year in school. But he loved to read. He began to study law when he was 25 years old. He had already been elected to the Illinois state legislature.

Lincoln was a good speaker and an honest person. He was a successful lawyer. Later he became a member of the House of Representatives in Washington, D.C.

Abraham Lincoln was elected President in 1860. At that time, slavery was still allowed in the Southeast Region and in Texas. People who owned slaves were afraid that Lincoln would put an end to slavery. They believed that slaves were needed for farming. Soon after the election, some states in the Southeast decided to start a new country.

Lincoln sent an army to keep them from doing this. A war started—between the North and the South. It is known as the Civil War. It lasted more than four years.

When the war was over, the Southeast Region and Texas were still part of our nation. And slavery was no longer allowed in the United States.

Abraham Lincoln

Complete each sentence. Circle the letter in front of the correct answer.

1. Under the homesteading plan, the government offered people moving to the Great Plains

    a. a covered wagon.
    b. land for farming.
    c. five hundred dollars.
    d. a brick house.

2. A sod house is made of

    a. bricks.
    b. wood.
    c. rocks.
    d. dirt.

3. The biggest cities in the North Central Region are near

    a. lakes.
    b. plateaus.
    c. mountains.
    d. oceans.

4. The city with the most people in the North Central Region is

    a. Chicago, Illinois.
    b. Detroit, Michigan.
    c. St. Louis, Missouri.
    d. Duluth, Minnesota.

5. The center of the American automobile business is

    a. Duluth, Minnesota.
    b. Chicago, Illinois.
    c. Detroit, Michigan.
    d. St. Louis, Missouri.

6. The biggest crop in the North Central Region is

    a. cattle.
    b. sugar.
    c. milk.
    d. corn.

THINKING AND WRITING Write a menu for a meal that has at least two food items made from corn.

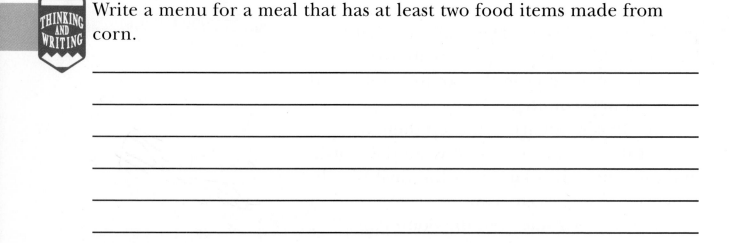

_____

_____

_____

_____

_____

_____

FACTS ABOUT THE STATES
OF THE NORTH CENTRAL REGION

STATE Origin of Name *Nickname(s)*	Capital	Population *(estimate)*	Rank	Bird	Flower
Illinois From Indian word meaning "group of superior men." *Land of Lincoln*	Springfield	11,697,000	**Pop.** 6 **Size** 24	Cardinal	Native violet
Indiana Named for area's American Indian groups. *Hoosier State*	Indianapolis	5,713,000	**Pop.** 14 **Size** 38	Cardinal	Peony
Iowa Named for Sioux Indians. It means "beautiful land." *Hawkeye State*	Des Moines	2,232,000	**Pop.** 30 **Size** 23	Eastern goldfinch	Wild rose
Kansas Named for the Kansa Indians. *Sunflower State* *Jayhawker State*	Topeka	2,531,000	**Pop.** 32 **Size** 13	Western meadowlark	Sunflower
Michigan Chippewa Indian word meaning "great water." *Wolverine State* *Water Wonderland*	Lansing	9,478,000	**Pop.** 8 **Size** 22	Robin	Apple blossom
Minnesota Sioux Indian word meaning "land of sky-tinted waters." *Land of 10,000 Lakes* *Gopher State*	St. Paul	4,517,000	**Pop.** 20 **Size** 14	Common loon	Pink and white lady's-slipper

STATE Origin of Name *Nickname(s)*	Capital	Population *(estimate)*	Rank	Bird	Flower
Missouri Missouri Indian word that probably means "people of the large canoes." *Show Me State* *Gateway to the West*	Jefferson City	5,234,000	**Pop**. 15 **Size** 18	Bluebird	Hawthorn
Nebraska Omaha Indian name for the Platte River. *Cornhusker State*	Lincoln	1,607,000	**Pop**. 36 **Size** 15	Western meadowlark	Goldenrod
North Dakota Sioux Indian word for "friends." *Sioux State* *Flickertail State*	Bismarck	635,000	**Pop**. 47 **Size** 17	Western meadowlark	Wild prairie rose
Ohio Iroquois Indian word for the Ohio River. *Buckeye State*	Columbus	11,091,000	**Pop**. 7 **Size** 35	Cardinal	Scarlet carnation
South Dakota Sioux Indian word for "friends." *Coyote State* *Sunshine State*	Pierre	715,000	**Pop**. 45 **Size** 16	Ring-necked pheasant	American pasqueflower
Wisconsin Chippewa Indian word for "gathering of the waters." *Badger State* *America's Dairyland*	Madison	5,021,000	**Pop**. 16 **Size** 25	Robin	Wood violet

Planning Routes

In this unit you learned that ships carry products from one Great Lakes port to another. But did you know that ships can travel from the Great Lakes all the way to the Atlantic Ocean? In the 1800s, people built canals to connect the Great Lakes to the St. Lawrence River, which flows into the Atlantic Ocean. Look at the map below.

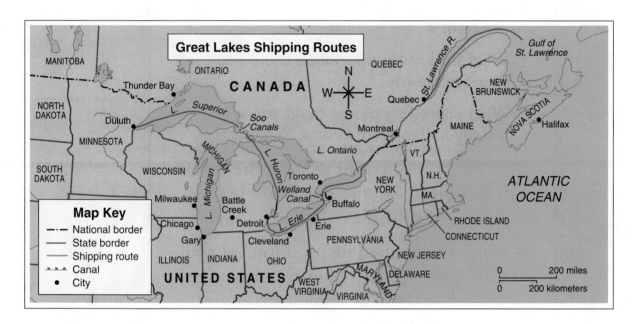

1. Which Great Lake is connected to the St. Lawrence River?

_____

2. Draw the route a ship would take to carry automobiles from Detroit, Michigan, to the port at Halifax, Nova Scotia.

3. Factories in Battle Creek, Michigan, need grain to make breakfast cereals. Ships carrying grain leave from Thunder Bay in Ontario, Canada. With your finger, trace a route from Thunder Bay to Detroit, Michigan. On which two Great Lakes will the ships travel?

_____

Now it's time to finish your unit project. Think about what you learned about the North Central Region city you chose. Talk with your team to answer questions like these.

- **How far away is the North Central Region city from where you live?**

- **What kind of transportation could you use to get to the city?**

- **What interesting places could you visit in the city in the North Central Region?**

Decide how you want to show the results of your project. Choose one of these ways or use one of your own ideas.

➤ Make a trip schedule for a tour of your team's city. Make a plan showing when you will leave your hometown and what kind of transportation you will take to the North Central Region. List all the places you will visit and their descriptions.

➤ On a map of the United States, draw a route from your community to the city your team chose. Use your list of places to make a tourist's guide to the city.

UNIT 5

The Rocky Mountain Region

Now we will visit the Rocky Mountain Region. This region is made up of six states. Hundreds of mountain peaks reach thousands of feet into the sky! You have probably seen the tall peaks of the Rocky Mountains in movies and photographs.

Unit 5 of this book will help you answer questions like these.

- What is the Continental Divide?
- Who were the mountain men?
- What kinds of jobs do people have in the Rocky Mountain Region?

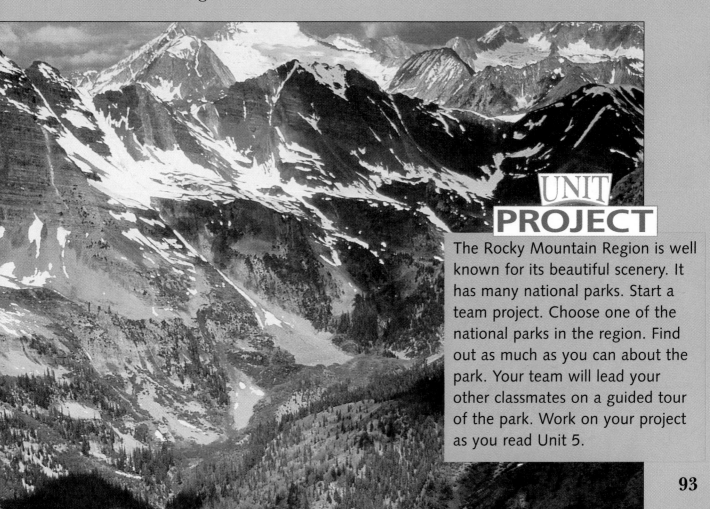

UNIT PROJECT

The Rocky Mountain Region is well known for its beautiful scenery. It has many national parks. Start a team project. Choose one of the national parks in the region. Find out as much as you can about the park. Your team will lead your other classmates on a guided tour of the park. Work on your project as you read Unit 5.

Geography of the Rocky Mountain Region

Where do you think the Rocky Mountain Region got its name? The answer is from one of the region's landforms. In this chapter, you'll find out about them.

Rocky Mountain States

 Look at the map. The capital cities are far apart. Use the distance scale to measure the distance between Helena, Montana, and Salt Lake City, Utah. Write the distance here.

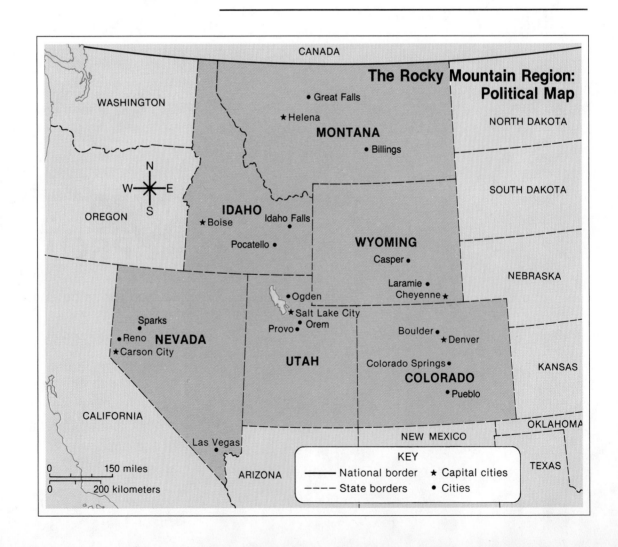

The Rocky Mountain Region: Political Map

CANADA

WASHINGTON

• Great Falls

★ Helena

MONTANA

• Billings

NORTH DAKOTA

SOUTH DAKOTA

OREGON

IDAHO Idaho Falls
★ Boise   •

Pocatello •

WYOMING

Casper •

Laramie •
Cheyenne ★

NEBRASKA

• Ogden
★ Salt Lake City
Provo • Orem

Sparks
•
• Reno **NEVADA**
★ Carson City

UTAH

Boulder •
★ Denver

Colorado Springs •
COLORADO
• Pueblo

KANSAS

CALIFORNIA

OKLAHOMA

Las Vegas •

NEW MEXICO

ARIZONA

KEY

0   150 miles

0   200 kilometers

National border   ★ Capital cities
State borders   • Cities

TEXAS

94

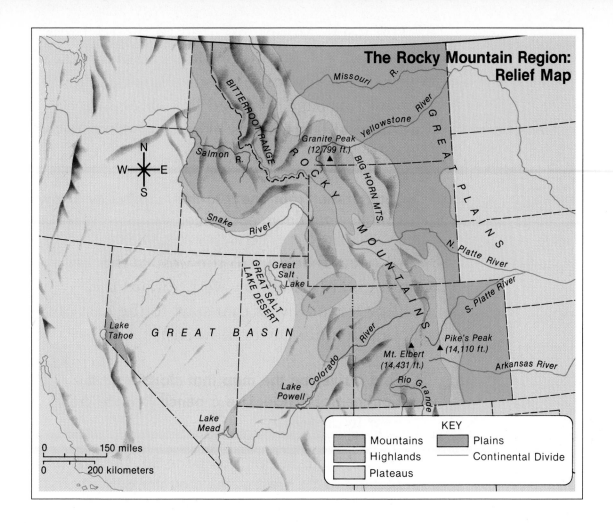

The Rocky Mountain Region: Relief Map

KEY
Mountains
Highlands
Plateaus
Plains
Continental Divide

Mountains, Canyons, Basins

The Rocky Mountains run through five of the six states of this region. The other state is on a high plateau. In Chapter 1 you learned that a plateau is a high, flat area of land.

 Look at the map key on this page. Find the color for plateaus. The Rocky Mountains do not run through which state? Write your answer here.

The Rocky Mountains are part of a long chain of mountains. This chain reaches from Alaska to the bottom of South America. Look at the map on page 96. You can see where part of the Rocky Mountains stretches down from Canada and across the United States.

The Rocky Mountains are like the roof of a house. When rain falls on one side of a roof, it rolls off that side of the house. Look at the map on this page. The red line shows the **Continental Divide.** It is like the highest part of a roof.

 Look at the "roof" next to the map below. Draw rain flowing down each side.

All rivers that start to the west of the Continental Divide flow west, toward the Pacific Ocean. Rivers that start to the east of the Continental Divide flow east.

 Find a river on the map that starts near the Continental Divide. Use a pencil to trace the river to an ocean.

Look at the relief map on page 95. Find the high plateau to the west of the mountains. Write its name here.

_____

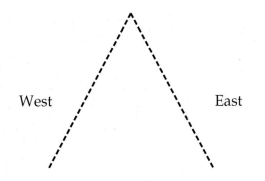

West   East

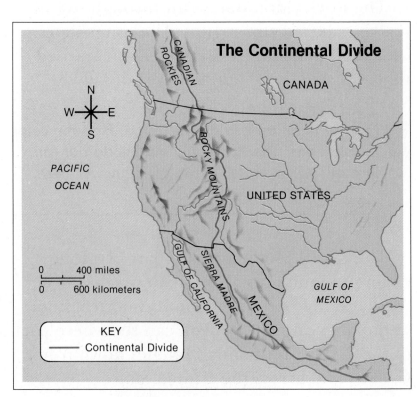

Glaciers move slowly at a rate of about a foot per day. As they move, they help shape the land. Glaciers have carved out lakes and deep valleys.

A **basin** is a landform shaped like a giant bowl. It has high sides all around. Once, the Great Basin was filled with water. There was a huge lake there. Over thousands of years, most of the water dried up. The water that is left now is so full of minerals, especially salt, that it is called the Great Salt Lake. Find the Great Salt Lake on the map on page 95.

It doesn't rain much in the Great Basin. Most of the water comes from ice and snow far up in the Rocky Mountains. Huge fields of ice and snow called **glaciers** lie on the highest slopes. Look at the photograph of the mountains on page 93. Even in summer, the mountains are covered with snow.

As the snow melts, the water flows into rivers. The rushing waters pull away dirt and rocks, forming **canyons.** Canyons are deep, narrow valleys formed after hundreds of thousands of years.

The rushing waters of the Colorado River carve away rocks. Some canyons look like castles.

 Look at the photograph on the right. What natural resource made the canyon? Write your answer here.

_____

 Write to the national park your team chose. Ask for information about the park. Ask about the park's most famous landforms. When you get the information, draw some of the landforms you like the most.

Machu Picchu

No one lives in the city of Machu Picchu any more. Visitors to Machu Picchu learn how the Inca lived hundreds of years ago.

As you learned, the Rockies are part of a long chain of mountains. The part of the chain that goes through South America is called the Andes Mountains.

The photograph shows you an old city high up in the Andes. It was called Machu Picchu. No one has lived in Machu Picchu for hundreds of years. American Indians called the Inca lived there. We know that the Inca were good builders because parts of their buildings still stand today. They also built a great network of roads to link parts of their kingdom together.

The Inca ruled a large region of the Andes from about 1400 to the early 1500s. They built cities and roads. They developed special ways to grow crops in the mountains. They worked hard to farm the steep mountainsides. The main crops of the Inca were corn, cotton, potatoes, and grain. The Inca were also very good at crafts. They dug for gold and silver and made beautiful jewelry and other items.

In the sixteenth century, Spanish explorers heard about the riches of the Inca and came to the Inca kingdom. The Spanish wanted to have the gold and silver for themselves. They tricked the Inca and killed their king. The Spanish soon took over the land of the Inca. Then they started Spanish colonies in South America.

Why do we think the Inca were good builders?

_____

Complete each sentence. Circle the letter in front of the correct answer.

1. The Rocky Mountains run through all the states in the region except
   a. Wyoming.
   b. Idaho.
   c. Nevada.
   d. Colorado.

2. The Rocky Mountain chain stretches down from Alaska all the way through to the bottom of
   a. Colorado.
   b. South America.
   c. Canada.
   d. Nevada.

3. Rivers that are west of the Continental Divide flow toward the
   a. Atlantic Ocean.
   b. Pacific Ocean.
   c. Great Basin.
   d. Great Lakes.

4. A basin is a landform that is shaped like a giant
   a. football.
   b. castle.
   c. bowl.
   d. canyon.

5. The Great Salt Lake is located in
   a. the Great Basin.
   b. the Rocky Mountains.
   c. the state of Colorado.
   d. the Continental Divide.

6. Deep, narrow valleys are called
   a. canyons.
   b. basins.
   c. mountains.
   d. plains.

 THINKING AND WRITING Find Sparks, Nevada, on the map on page 94. Use what you learned in this chapter to describe what it might be like to live there.

_____

_____

_____

_____

_____

People of the Rocky Mountain Region

In this chapter you'll find out how people in the Rocky Mountain Region live today. But first let's meet one group who learned how to live in the region more than 150 years ago.

Long Ago in the Rockies: The Mountain Men

Jed Smith was born in New York State in 1799. As a boy he learned how to live in the woods. At the age of 22, Jed headed west in search of adventure. He joined a group of explorers.

What do you think Jed Smith learned to do? Write your answer here.

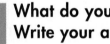

_____

Jed was very brave. Once, when he was in South Dakota, he was attacked by a very large bear. Jed was almost killed, but a month later he was strong enough to walk.

In the Rocky Mountains, Jed was a trapper. He caught animals and sold them for their fur. There were hundreds of men like Jed. They called themselves mountain men.

The mountain men had to spend a lot of time alone. They would hunt for 11 months. Then, in late summer, they would take the furs to a place where they could sell them.

Mountain men made their own clothes from the skins of animals they killed.

The most important thing Jed owned was his gun. He used it to shoot animals for food. He also used it to keep large animals away. Next to his gun and his knife, a fur trapper like Jed needed his traps. He needed traps to catch beavers. He sold beaver furs to make a little bit of money.

Making money wasn't the most important thing to mountain men. Just staying alive in the wilderness wasn't easy. There were no doctors and no stores that sold food. Many mountain men learned the skills they needed to live in the Rocky Mountain Region from American Indians who lived there.

Most of the mountain men lived in the Rockies because they loved the mountains. They loved their free outdoor life.

By the early 1840s, the fur business was ending. Many mountain men built houses in the region. Others became guides for wagon trains bringing new **settlers** to the area. Settlers are people who go to live in a new part of a country. Today there are no mountain men. They are part of the history of the Rocky Mountain Region.

 Why do you think the mountain men were good guides for the new settlers?

_____

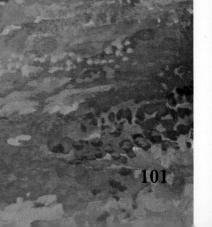

101

Hundreds of years ago, American Indians called the Anasazi built their homes in canyon walls. The Anasazi disappeared before the Europeans came to America.

American Indians in the Region

The mountain men came to the Rocky Mountain Region in the 1820s. Small groups of American Indians had been living in the region for a long time.

During the 1800s, many new settlers came to the region. The American Indians and the settlers had different ideas about how to use the land. There were many battles. The United States government finally moved the Indians off the land and onto **reservations.** A reservation is land set aside by the government where American Indian groups can live. The reservations were often far from where the groups had been living. The land was not good for farming or hunting. Life on reservations was very hard.

Today, some American Indians still live on reservations in the Rocky Mountain Region and in other areas of the country. But American Indians do not have to live on reservations any more. Like other citizens of the United States, they can live where they choose.

Why was life hard on the early reservations?

Where Do People Live in the Region?

Today, about nine million people live in the Rocky Mountain Region. It has the smallest population of all the regions in the United States. As in the other regions of the United States, most people in the Rocky Mountain Region live in cities. The city with the largest population is Denver, Colorado.

In the 1860s, Denver was a small town. People called **miners** were looking for gold and silver in the area. By the 1880s, a railroad had been built to Denver. More people and businesses moved there. Today, Denver is a major business and transportation center.

Denver is only ten miles from the Rockies. Temperatures are usually cooler up in the mountains than down on the plains. Look at the **line graph** below. A line graph shows how something changes over time. This line graph shows what the temperatures are like in Denver during the year.

What are the warmest and coldest months in Denver? Write your answer here.

_____

Denver is the largest city in the Rocky Mountain Region.

MONTHLY NORMAL TEMPERATURE IN DENVER, COLORADO

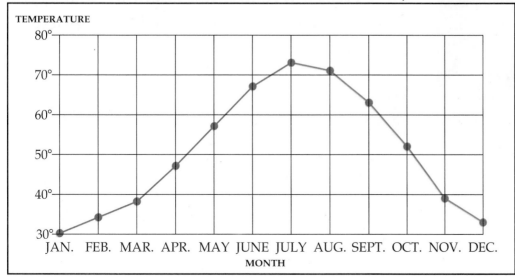

Another important city is near the Great Salt Lake. It is Salt Lake City.

Find Salt Lake City on the map on page 94. What state is it in? Write the state here.

_____

Salt Lake City was started in 1847 by a religious group called the **Mormons.** Like the Pilgrims, they wanted their own land and a place to worship. They worked hard and turned the dry lands into farms. Salt Lake City is still the center of the Mormon religion. More than two out of every three people who live in Utah are Mormons.

Cheyenne, Wyoming, has a population of only 50,000 people. Still, it is one of the biggest cities in the whole Rocky Mountain Region. Every year people from all over the region visit Cheyenne. Many go to watch the Frontier Days **Rodeo.** A rodeo is a contest for cowboys and cowgirls. At rodeos they get a chance to show the skills they use in their jobs on cattle ranches.

Nevada has the fastest growing population in the nation. Lots of new businesses have opened in Nevada because running a business there costs less than it does in other states. Many of the new businesses make things like computers.

The center of downtown Salt Lake City is Temple Square. The Mormon Temple, or church, is there. How many towers does it have?

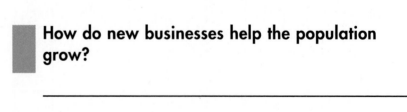

How do new businesses help the population grow?

_____

_____

_____

104

Working in the Rocky Mountain Region

There are lots of ranches in the eastern part of the region. The Great Plains come right up to the mountains there. The land there is good for raising cattle.

 Look at the maps on pages 94 and 95. What three states do you think are best for ranching? Write your answer here.

_____

_____

People in the region also raise a lot of sheep. Sheep can live in the mountains where the land is not good for farming or raising cattle.

People do some farming in the areas that are not in the mountains. Idaho is famous for growing potatoes. Idaho grows more potatoes than any other state! Farmers in Idaho and Montana also grow wheat and other grains.

Raising cattle is an important business in the Rocky Mountain Region.

Miners look for minerals in the earth.

Yellowstone National Park in Wyoming contains many natural wonders such as waterfalls, canyons, and geysers—natural fountains that shoot hot water and steam high into the air.

Look at the photograph above. The men are miners looking for minerals in the earth. About 150 years ago, large amounts of minerals were discovered in the region. Most of our gold and silver comes from this region.

Some of the mountains, lakes, rivers, and canyons are a resource because they are so beautiful. Each year millions of tourists visit the 11 national parks in the region. Park visitors can hike or simply enjoy the scenery.

Many people in the Rocky Mountain Region have tourism jobs. These include car rental agent, souvenir seller, and park ranger. These jobs are also service jobs. Like other regions of the country, more people in the region have service jobs than any other kind of job.

What are three important jobs in the region? Write your answer here.

_____

_____

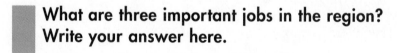

How can people enjoy the national park you chose to study? Find out what activities the park offers. What sounds like the most fun?

Chief Joseph

During the 1800s, many American Indians lost their homes. Over and over, the United States government forced American Indians to give their lands to settlers and move to reservations.

This happened in the Rocky Mountain Region, too. One group that lost their land was the Nez Perce. Their land was in the states of Idaho, Oregon, and Washington.

In the 1870s, some settlers wanted the rich lands for farms. The United States government ordered the Nez Perce to leave their villages. The government wanted them to go to a small reservation in Idaho.

The Nez Perce were led by a great chief named Joseph. He tried to get the United States government to let the Nez Perce stay. Then fighting started.

Chief Joseph tried to lead his group to safety in Canada. His people walked 1,600 miles and fought many battles all winter. They were finally caught by the United States Army near Canada.

The Nez Perce were taken to Oklahoma, not Idaho. The next year Chief Joseph went to Washington, D.C., to ask for the right to return to the Rocky Mountains. He said, "The Earth is the mother of all people, and all people should have equal rights upon it. Let me be a free man and I will obey every law."

Chief Joseph

What do you think Chief Joseph wanted to be free to do? Write your answer here.

_____

_____

Complete each sentence. Circle the letter in front of the correct answer.

1. People who go to live in a new part of a country are called
   a. guides.
   b. mountain men.
   c. settlers.
   d. miners.

2. Of all the regions in the United States, the Rocky Mountain Region has the
   a. most people.
   b. fewest people.
   c. best land for farming.
   d. best land for houses.

3. Most people in the region live
   a. in small towns.
   b. in cities.
   c. on farms.
   d. on ranches.

4. In the 1800s, the United States government forced American Indians to move to
   a. reservations.
   b. cities.
   c. farms.
   d. national parks.

5. Salt Lake City was begun by a group of settlers called
   a. American Indians.
   b. cowboys.
   c. mountain men.
   d. Mormons.

6. Many people in the region have
   a. tourism jobs.
   b. teaching jobs.
   c. fishing jobs.
   d. ship-building jobs.

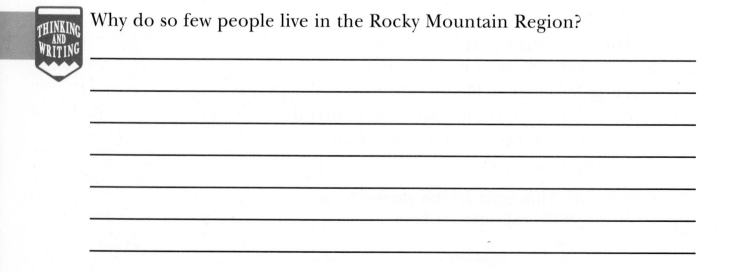

THINKING AND WRITING Why do so few people live in the Rocky Mountain Region?

_____

_____

_____

_____

_____

_____

_____

FACTS ABOUT THE STATES OF THE ROCKY MOUNTAIN REGION

STATE Origin of Name Nickname(s)	Capital	Population (estimate)	Rank	Bird	Flower
Colorado Spanish word for red, the color of the Colorado River. *Centennial State*	Denver	3,566,000	**Pop.** 26 **Size** 8	Lark bunting	Rocky Mountain columbine
Idaho Meaning unknown. *Gem State* *Spud State*	Boise	1,099,000	**Pop.** 42 **Size** 11	Mountain bluebird	Syringa (mock orange)
Montana Spanish word for mountain. *Treasure State*	Helena	839,000	**Pop.** 44 **Size** 4	Western meadowlark	Bitterroot
Nevada Spanish word for snow covered. *Silver State*	Carson City	1,389,000	**Pop.** 39 **Size** 7	Mountain bluebird	Sagebrush
Utah Named for the Ute Indians. *Beehive State*	Salt Lake City	1,879,301	**Pop.** 35 **Size** 12	Seagull	Sego lily
Wyoming Delaware Indian word, means "at the great plains." *Equality State* *Cowboy State*	Cheyenne	469,210	**Pop.** 50 **Size** 9	Meadowlark	Indian paintbrush

Reading a Line Graph

Large numbers of settlers first began coming to Nevada in 1859 when silver was discovered there. The line graph below shows how Nevada's population has changed since 1870.

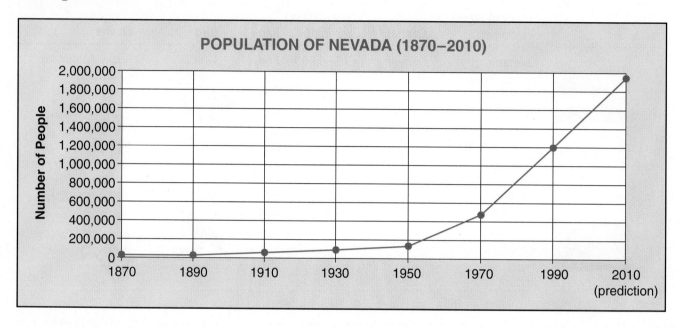

POPULATION OF NEVADA (1870–2010)

1. Circle the answer that tells what happened to Nevada's population between 1870 and 1990.

   It got bigger.   It stayed the same.   It got smaller.

2. When was Nevada's population about 200,000?

   _____

3. What was the population of Nevada in 1990?

   _____

4. Did the population grow more between 1930 and 1950 or between 1970 and 1990?

   _____

5. How would a line graph look for a town whose population got smaller?

   _____

Now it's time to finish your unit project. Think about what you learned about your team's national park. Talk with your team to answer questions like these.

- **What makes the national park an interesting place to visit?**

- **What special landforms does the park have?**

- **What kinds of things can you do at the park?**

Decide how you want to show the results of your project. Choose one of these ways or use one of your own ideas.

➤ Choose a part of the classroom to be your park's visitor center. Invite your classmates to the visitor center. On the walls of the visitor center, display the pictures you drew. Each team member can be a park ranger and tell the class something about the park.

➤ Invite another class to a tour of the parks of the Rocky Mountain Region. Each team's park will be a stop on the tour. When the class visits your team's park, prepare to give a presentation about the park. Be ready to answer questions!

Land, Rivers, and Climate

The land of the Southwest looks like a set of stairs. The lowest step is the Coastal Plain. Look at the map below. Find the words *Coastal Plain* near the Gulf of Mexico.

The Great Plains are the middle step. They are higher than the Coastal Plains, but lower than highlands or mountains.

 Arizona and New Mexico are the top step. Look at the map. What landforms make up these states? Write your answer here.

_____

There are many rivers on the plains of Texas. There is only one major river in the highlands and plateaus of Arizona. It is the Colorado River. A long time ago the Colorado River carved out the Grand Canyon. The Grand Canyon is a mile deep!

 Find the Grand Canyon and Colorado River on the map. Circle the Grand Canyon.

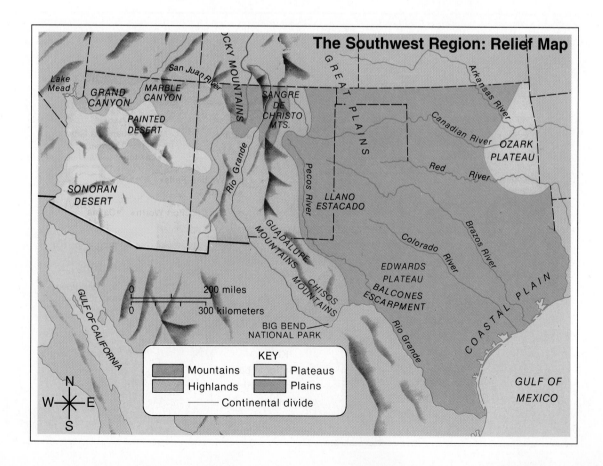

The Southwest Region: Relief Map

Lake Mead · GRAND CANYON · MARBLE CANYON · San Juan River · ROCKY MOUNTAINS · SANGRE DE CHRISTO MTS. · GREAT PLAINS · Arkansas River · Canadian River · OZARK PLATEAU · PAINTED DESERT · Rio Grande · Pecos River · Red River · SONORAN DESERT · LLANO ESTACADO · Colorado River · Brazos River · GUADALUPE MOUNTAINS · CHISOS MOUNTAINS · EDWARDS PLATEAU · BALCONES ESCARPMENT · COASTAL PLAIN · GULF OF CALIFORNIA · 200 miles · 300 kilometers · BIG BEND NATIONAL PARK · Rio Grande · GULF OF MEXICO

KEY
- Mountains
- Highlands
- Plateaus
- Plains
- — Continental divide

W N E S

Parts of the Southwest are known for being hot and sunny. The Southwest is part of the Sunbelt. But this does not mean that the whole region has the same climate. On a day when oranges are growing in the south of Texas, it may be snowing in the north of Texas. Texas is a big state!

 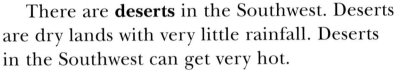 **Turn back to the climate map on page 13. Find Texas. How many climate areas does it have? Write your answer here.**

_____

These crops in Arizona could not grow without the help of irrigation.

There are **deserts** in the Southwest. Deserts are dry lands with very little rainfall. Deserts in the Southwest can get very hot.

Desert plants have long roots that reach deep into the ground where there is water. Desert animals hide from the strong sun. They look for food and water at night.

People have found ways to bring water from far away to the desert. Watering crops by bringing water to an area where it is in short supply is called **irrigation.** With the help of irrigation, farmers can grow cotton, vegetables, and other crops.

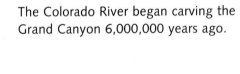

The Colorado River began carving the Grand Canyon 6,000,000 years ago.

UNIT PROJECT Tip Find out where the group of American Indians you chose lived before settlers arrived. Write a scene for your play about their life during that time.

Mexico

Mexico is the United States' neighbor to the south. Look at the map on page 113. Find Mexico. Texas, New Mexico, and Arizona are on the border of Mexico.

Mexico has many different landforms. Like farmers in the Southwest, Mexican farmers use irrigation to grow crops in dry areas.

Mexico also has factories that make car parts, electronics, computers, and other products. Oil is another important product of Mexico. The United States buys a lot of oil from Mexico.

Many people live in Mexico. The biggest city in North America is in Mexico. It is Mexico City, the capital of Mexico. More than 20 million people live in Mexico City. That's three times as many people as in New York City!

List two ways that Mexico and the Southwest Region are alike.

Many important businesses are located in Mexico's capital, Mexico City.

CHAPTER ✓ CHECKUP

Complete each sentence. Circle the letter in front of the correct answer.

1. More than half of the land in the Southwest is

   a. mountains.
   b. plateaus.
   c. flat plains.
   d. highlands.

2. The largest state in the Southwest is

   a. Arizona.
   b. New Mexico.
   c. Oklahoma.
   d. Texas.

3. Most of the rivers in the Southwest are in the

   a. mountains.
   b. plains.
   c. deserts.
   d. highlands.

4. The Grand Canyon was carved by

   a. the Colorado River.
   b. the desert.
   c. American Indians.
   d. irrigation.

5. Deserts are lands that have very little

   a. warm air.
   b. mountains.
   c. rainfall.
   d. sunshine.

6. When farmers bring water to dry land from far away, it is called

   a. a coastal plain.
   b. irrigation.
   c. farming.
   d. a desert.

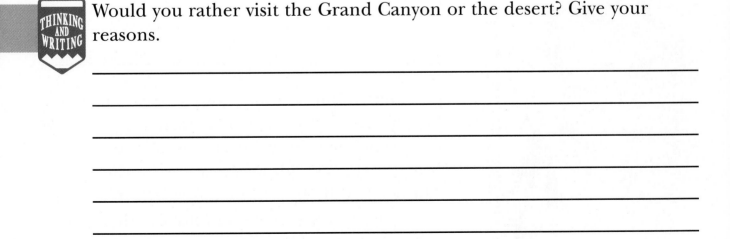

THINKING AND WRITING Would you rather visit the Grand Canyon or the desert? Give your reasons.

_____

_____

_____

_____

_____

_____

_____

_____

People of the Southwest Region

Many people settled in the Southwest in the past. Today many people are still moving there. But who were the very first people to live in the region? American Indian groups arrived thousands of years ago.

Long Ago: The Comanche

The Comanche once ruled the plains. They were great hunters and fighters. They lived in small groups. They moved to find food. In summer they followed the herds of deer and buffalo across the plains. They dried some of the meat to eat during the winter.

For hundreds of years, Comanche children learned the same lessons. Fathers taught sons to hunt. Mothers taught daughters to prepare food and clothing from buffalo and deer.

Why do you think the Comanche dried meat for the winter? Write your answer here.

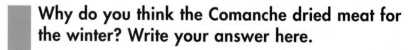

_____

_____

Then, about 300 years ago, a great change began. Other people arrived from Spain. They were ranchers who came to raise cattle. They brought horses with them to the Southwest. These were the first horses in North America.

Once the Comanche had horses, their way of life changed. They became great riders. Now it was easier to follow and hunt the buffalo herds.

Horses also made the Comanche strong in war. On horseback they were able to win more battles. By 1800 they ruled a large part of the Southwest.

Soon thousands of settlers moved to Texas. They moved there because they wanted to build farms and ranches.

The Comanche tried to make the settlers leave. Then United States soldiers attacked Comanche camps. The fighting went on for a long time. But the guns and soldiers did not beat the Comanche.

The Comanche were beaten by sickness. The settlers brought sicknesses from Europe. The Comanche had never had these sicknesses before. Thousands died. In the early 1800s, there had been 30,000 Comanche. Fifty years later there were only half as many.

About how many Comanche were there in 1850? Write your answer here.

_____

The Comanche were also beaten by the buffalo hunters with guns. The hunters killed the animals that the Comanche needed for food and clothing. These hunters killed as many buffalo as they could. In just a few years, the great buffalo herds were gone.

In 1875 the last Comanche were moved to a reservation. They were no longer allowed to move across the plains.

What two "enemies" hurt the Comanche most? Write your answer here.

_____

Who Are the People of the Region?

About 27 million people live in the four southwestern states. There are more American Indians and Mexican Americans in the Southwest Region than in any other region.

American Indian groups arrived in the Southwest long ago. The Navajo and Pueblo were living in the Southwest by the year 1300.

What groups of people lived in the Southwest Region about 700 years ago? Write your answer here.

the Pueblo and Navajo

During the early 1800s, most of what is now Oklahoma was known as Indian Territory. The United States government had set aside this land for American Indians. Many American Indians from different parts of the country had been forced to settle in Indian Territory.

By the 1880s many settlers had come and set up cattle ranches all around Indian Territory. The settlers told the government they wanted the land in Indian Territory. The government told the American Indians they could sell the land. Many American Indians sold their land in Oklahoma.

In 1889 the government held a Land Rush—a race to claim land that had once been Indian Territory. Over 50,000 settlers entered Oklahoma in one day to get the land.

Today a large number of American Indians live in the Southwest. Many live on reservations in the region. The Navajo reservation covers parts of Arizona, New Mexico, and Utah. It is the largest American Indian reservation in the United States.

These students are taking a class at Navajo Community College, located on the Navajo reservation in Tsaile, Arizona. It is the first college owned and operated by American Indians.

People from Spain arrived in the Southwest in the 1500s. They built a colony in New Mexico in 1598, more than 20 years before the Pilgrims landed in the Northeast.

Spanish-speaking people have lived in the Southwest for hundreds of years. Until about 150 years ago, most of the Southwest was part of Mexico or a colony of Spain. All through the 1900s, thousands of Mexicans moved to the Southwest. Today, Mexican Americans make up almost one fourth of the population of the Southwest.

The people of Santa Fe, New Mexico, have a Spanish festival every fall. They have had this festival for almost 300 years.

■ **Look at the time line at the bottom of the page. A time line is a line that shows a number of years. Marks on the line stand for events that happened during those years.**

Some events of the Southwest Region are shown on the time line. This time line covers 600 years. Each small part of the time line stands for 100 years.

Write *1889* where it belongs on the time line. Draw a line to the words that go with it.

How many years passed between the time when the first Spanish colony was started and the Land Rush? Write your answer here.

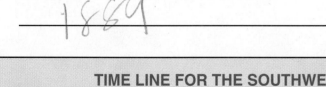

1889

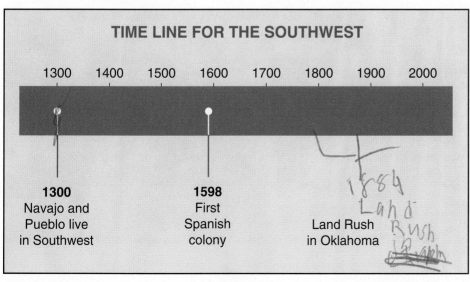

TIME LINE FOR THE SOUTHWEST

| 1300 | 1400 | 1500 | 1600 | 1700 | 1800 | 1900 | 2000 |

1300
Navajo and Pueblo live in Southwest

1598
First Spanish colony

Land Rush in Oklahoma

1889
Land Rush in

121

Where Do People Live in the Region?

You have learned that there are deserts in the Southwest. There is not much water. Most people in the Southwest live in cities.

The city of San Antonio is by a river on the Texas plains. It began as a farming village. Because the weather is so warm there, farmers grow crops all year round.

Houston, Texas, is also on a river. The river flows into the Gulf of Mexico. Houston became a major port after oil was discovered in Texas.

Oil is very important to many of the cities in the Southwest. Tulsa, Oklahoma, was an American Indian farming village. After oil was discovered there, it became a big business center. Now more than 350 oil companies have their offices there.

Oil is a very important business in Tulsa, Oklahoma, but the city also has many factories that make goods such as heaters, transportation equipment, and glass products.

 What business is important to both Texas and Oklahoma?

_____

122

Some southwestern cities were built near old roads or trails. Many of these had been used by travelers for centuries. The city of Albuquerque started along a road. Later a railroad was built across New Mexico. Now Albuquerque is the largest city in the state.

How do you think the railroad helped Albuquerque grow? Write your answer here.

_____

_____

Oklahoma City was one of the first towns settled during the Land Rush of 1889. Oil was discovered under the city in 1928. The city grew very fast after that.

Many cities in the Southwest have Spanish names. That is usually because they were started by the early Spanish settlers. Some houses in southwestern cities look like houses in Mexico. People often eat Mexican food and play Mexican music. The Southwest also has the largest Mexican American population in the country.

The Red Earth Festival takes place in Oklahoma City, Oklahoma. Oklahoma is the home of more than 60 different American Indian groups.

123

Traveling in the Southwest Region

How do drivers find the way to places they have never been before? Most of the time, they use road maps. Some maps also show places of special interest to travelers.

For example, pretend you're traveling through Oklahoma. You would like to find a campground where you can spend the night.

This woman kneels by the water in Tsa-La-Gi, an Indian village near Jahlequah, Oklahoma, that has been made to look the way it did long ago.

 Look at the road map below. It shows part of Oklahoma. Look at the map key. Find the symbol for campground. Circle the campground you would reach by traveling on Interstate Highway 40.

Now pretend you are traveling from the town of Chandler to the town of Goldsby. Find the town of Chandler in the northeast corner of the road map. Next, find the town of Goldsby. Now trace the roads you would follow to drive from Chandler to Goldsby.

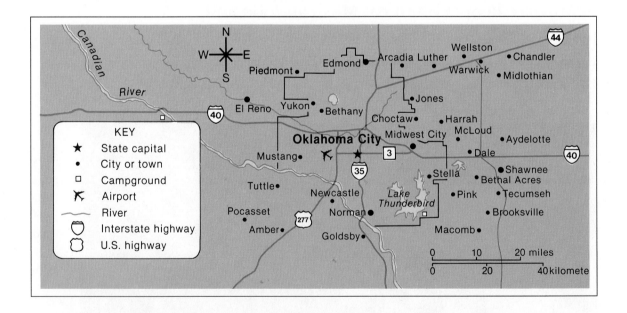

Write another scene for your play. How does the American Indian group your team is studying live today? Do some members of the group live on a reservation in the Southwest? If so, locate the reservation on a map.

Working in the Southwest Region

Ranching was the first business in the Southwest. People from Spain started raising cattle in Texas by the 1700s.

Ranching became more important as the United States grew. One Texas ranch grew bigger than the state of Rhode Island!

There were no railroads in Texas in the early 1800s. So ranchers had to walk the cattle north to cities where there were railroads. These cattle drives were hundreds of miles long and very dangerous.

In the late 1800s, railroads were built to Texas. The long cattle drives were over. But cattle ranching is still an important business in Texas today.

Why do you think railroads ended the need for the cattle drives?

_____

_____

Ranchers need horses so that they can herd their cattle.

Around 1900 a new business grew up in the Southwest—oil. The states of Texas and Oklahoma produce a lot of oil.

Oil is used to make gasoline and other products. Cars, planes, and ships need gas and oil to be able to move. Homes and buildings are heated with oil. Plastics and many other products are made from oil.

Usually, oil is found far under the ground. Special wells are needed to pump it out. Then it must go to a place called a **refinery.** In a refinery, the oil is cleaned and made into different products.

Today there are many jobs in the oil business. What jobs will the Southwest have in the future? New jobs usually come from **research.** Research means studying things and finding out about them.

Research is often done by businesses and universities. Research scientists often solve problems by finding better ways to do things. For example, we know we have to be careful with our natural resources. One thing researchers in the Southwest work on is new ways to use less oil. They study other types of energy that can be used. Have you ever heard of **solar energy?** Solar energy uses the heat of the sun instead of oil to heat homes.

 If you did research, what would you want to study? Write your answer here.

_____

Many people in the Southwest have service jobs. Like other regions of the United States, the Southwest needs teachers, doctors, salespeople, and other service workers.

Oil refineries have miles of pipes for carrying the oil.

César Chávez spent his life trying to improve working conditions on farms in the West and Southwest.

César Chávez was born in Yuma, Arizona, in 1927. His grandfather had come from Mexico to start a farm in Arizona. When César was ten, the family lost their farm. They had to travel from farm to farm to find work. Like many other farm workers, the Chávez family lived in a small shack and worked long hours for low pay.

When César Chávez grew up, he wanted to get better conditions for farm workers. He started a **labor union.** A labor union is a group of workers who try to get better working conditions and pay for its members.

César Chávez

At first many farm workers were afraid they would lose their jobs if they joined the union. But some workers joined, and the union grew. The union asked owners of grape farms to increase their workers' pay. The owners refused, so the union called a **strike.** A strike means the stopping of work. The workers stopped picking grapes until their demands were met.

Chávez asked people who were not farm workers to **boycott** grapes until the strike ended. When people boycott they refuse to buy a product. The grape farm owners lost a lot of money because so many people did not buy grapes. Finally the owners agreed to the union's demands.

What do labor unions try to get for their members?

_____

Complete each sentence. Circle the letter in front of the correct answer.

1. The first people to live in the Southwest were

  a. Spaniards.
  b. American Indians.
  c. settlers.
  d. Mexican Americans.

2. The Comanche were able to hunt better when they got

  a. sick.
  b. reservations.
  c. settlers.
  d. horses.

3. The largest American Indian reservation in the United States is that of the

  a. Comanche.
  b. Pueblo.
  c. Sioux.
  d. Navajo.

4. To get their cattle to market, ranches had cattle drives to get to

  a. Texas.
  b. railroads.
  c. Mexico.
  d. rivers.

5. The states of Texas and Oklahoma produce a lot of

  a. soil.
  b. steel.
  c. electricity.
  d. oil.

6. One thing research scientists do is

  a. look for gold.
  b. move to Oklahoma.
  c. find better ways to do things.
  d. go on cattle drives.

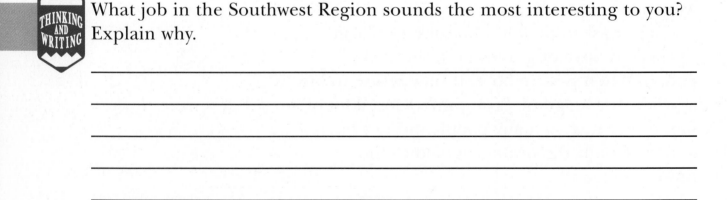

THINKING AND WRITING What job in the Southwest Region sounds the most interesting to you? Explain why.

_____

_____

_____

_____

_____

_____

_____

FACTS ABOUT THE STATES
OF THE SOUTHWEST REGION

STATE Origin of Name *Nickname(s)*	Capital	Population *(estimate)*	Rank	Bird	Flower
Arizona Papago Indian word meaning "place of little springs." *Grand Canyon State* *Sunset State* *Apache State*	Phoenix	3,936,000	**Pop.** 24 **Size** 6	Cactus wren	Saguaro (giant cactus)
New Mexico Named for Mexitli, an Aztec Indian god. *Land of Enchantment* *Sunshine State*	Santa Fe	1,616,000	**Pop.** 37 **Size** 5	Roadrunner	Yucca
Oklahoma Choctaw Indian word. *Okla* means "people," *homma* means "red." *Sooner State*	Oklahoma City	3,231,000	**Pop.** 28 **Size** 19	Scissor-tailed flycatcher	Mistletoe
Texas From *tejas*, Spanish name for Hasina Indians. Word meant "friends" or "allies." *Lone Star State*	Austin	18,031,000	**Pop.** 3 **Size** 2	Mockingbird	Bluebonnet

Unit 6 Skill Builder

Reading a Road Map

Look at the road map of part of New Mexico. There is often more than one road you can take to the same place. Road maps can show you the shortest way.

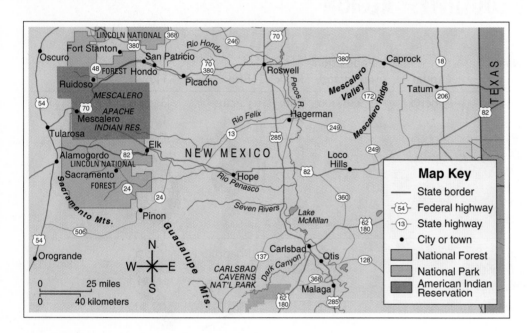

1. What two kinds of roads appear on the map?

   _____

2. Which federal highway goes through the Mescalero Apache Indian Reservation?

   _____

3. What road would you take to travel from Roswell to Caprock? What direction would you travel?

   _____

4. Someone tells you about the underground caves at Carlsbad Caverns National Park. List the roads you would take from Caprock to Carlsbad Caverns.

   _____

Now it's time to finish your unit project. Think about what you learned about the American Indian group your team studied. Talk with your team about answers to questions like these.

- **Where did the American Indian group live before settlers arrived?**

- **What events changed the lives of American Indians? How did those events affect your group?**

- **How do members of the group live today?**

Decide how you want to present your play. Use one of these ways or use an idea of your own.

➤ With your team, practice acting out the scenes you developed. When you are ready, invite the class to watch your play.

➤ Work together with your team to draw the way you think scenes of your play would look with costumes and scenery. Have each team member read part of the play as you display the pictures you drew.

The Pacific Region

The last region you'll visit is the Pacific Region. The five states in the Pacific Region all border the Pacific Ocean. In this unit you'll visit the warmest and the coldest states. And you'll discover communities of people from every part of the world. To see the whole region you have to travel farther north, south, and west than any of the places you have visited.

This unit will help you answer questions like these about the Pacific Region.

- Why do earthquakes occur in the Pacific Region?

- What was the Gold Rush?

- What kinds of jobs are there in the Pacific Region?

UNIT PROJECT

Start a team project. Choose one of the states of the Pacific Region. Find out more about the state. Develop a travel guide that gives interesting information for your state.

CHAPTER 14

Geography of the Pacific Region

The Pacific Region is the only region where two of the states are separated from the rest of the United States. That is why its geography is the most varied and unusual of any region.

The West Coast States

Three of the Pacific Region states are called the West Coast states. Find them on the map at the left. Trace the edges of the three states with a pencil or crayon.

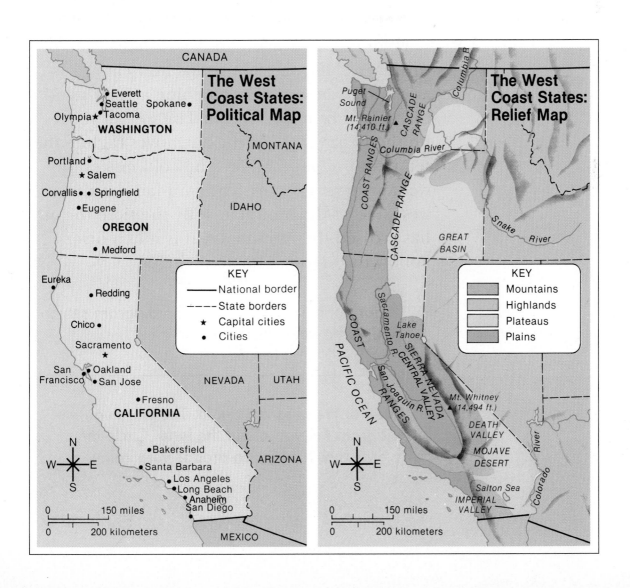

The West Coast States: Political Map

CANADA
• Everett
• Seattle   Spokane •
Olympia ★ • Tacoma
WASHINGTON
MONTANA
Portland •
★ Salem
Corvallis • • Springfield
• Eugene
OREGON
IDAHO
• Medford
Eureka
• Redding
Chico •
Sacramento
★
San   • Oakland
Francisco • San Jose
NEVADA   UTAH
• Fresno
CALIFORNIA

KEY
— National border
- - - State borders
★ Capital cities
• Cities

N
W ★ E
S
• Bakersfield
• Santa Barbara
ARIZONA
• Los Angeles
• Long Beach
• Anaheim
San Diego

0   150 miles
0   200 kilometers
MEXICO

The West Coast States: Relief Map

Columbia R.
Puget Sound
Mt. Rainier
(14,410 ft.)
CASCADE RANGE
Columbia River
COAST RANGES
CASCADE RANGE
Snake River
GREAT BASIN
Sacramento R.
Lake Tahoe
COAST
PACIFIC OCEAN
RANGES
CENTRAL VALLEY
San Joaquin R.
SIERRA NEVADA
Mt. Whitney
(14,494 ft.)
DEATH VALLEY
MOJAVE DESERT
Colorado River
Salton Sea
IMPERIAL VALLEY

KEY
Mountains
Highlands
Plateaus
Plains

N
W ★ E
S

0   150 miles
0   200 kilometers

133

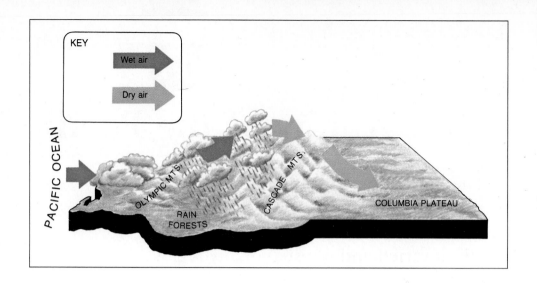

All three states have mild climates. This is because the Pacific Ocean carries warm water and warm breezes from the south. They help keep the temperatures mild. They also cause more rain to fall in Oregon and Washington.

A **diagram** shows how something is made or how something works. Look at the diagram on this page. This diagram shows how climate is affected by mountains. The blue arrows stand for wet air from the ocean. The wet air moves up the mountains. As the air moves higher, the temperature gets colder. The cold makes the wet air turn into rain. The rain falls on the west side of the mountains. By the time the air has crossed the mountains, it is much drier. Follow the arrows with your finger.

 What do the red arrows on the diagram stand for? Write your answer here.

ary here

Look at the diagram again. The words on the diagram tell you about the land. Circle the words that tell you an area is very rainy.

Earthquakes

People were sound asleep when the ground began to shake. Some people were thrown out of their beds! Lamps fell and set fire to houses. In a few hours, 3,000 people had died and 28,000 buildings had been destroyed.

This happened in the **earthquake** that hit San Francisco, California, in 1906. An earthquake is a strong shaking of the ground.

In the United States, most earthquakes happen in the Pacific Region. This is because two gigantic areas of land meet there. One is under the Pacific Ocean. The other is under the West Coast. If one of them moves against the other, it causes the ground nearby to shake. The place where the two land areas meet is called a **fault**.

Most earthquakes in the Pacific Region are very small. The strongest earthquake in North America took place in Alaska in 1964. Scientists have equipment to measure how strong earthquakes are. They use a special scale called a Richter scale to measure the earthquake. The highest Richter scale ever measured was 8.9. The 1906 San Francisco earthquake measured 8.3.

In a lab, this scientist studies information about earthquakes.

What is an earthquake?

_____

This is what part of San Francisco looked like after the 1906 earthquake.

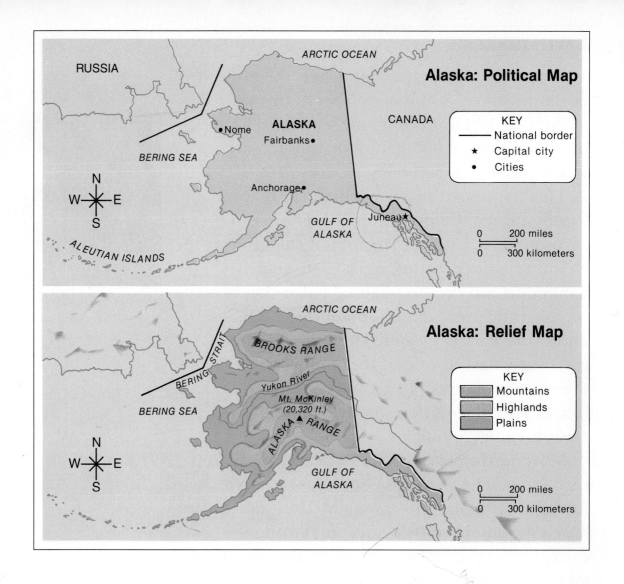

Alaska: Political Map

RUSSIA

ARCTIC OCEAN

ALASKA

CANADA

•Nome

Fairbanks•

BERING SEA

Anchorage•

ALEUTIAN ISLANDS

GULF OF
ALASKA

Juneau★

KEY
— National border
★ Capital city
• Cities

0   200 miles
0   300 kilometers

Alaska: Relief Map

ARCTIC OCEAN

BROOKS RANGE

BERING STRAIT

Yukon River

Mt. McKinley
(20,320 ft.)

ALASKA RANGE

BERING SEA

GULF OF
ALASKA

KEY
Mountains
Highlands
Plains

0   200 miles
0   300 kilometers

Alaska

Alaska is our largest state. To reach Alaska from the state of Washington, you have to travel hundreds of miles north through Canada.

 Look at the political map. Find the capital of Alaska and circle its name.

Now look at the relief map. Find the plains in northern Alaska. This land is **tundra**—land that is too cold for trees to grow. Tundra soil is almost always frozen. Not all of Alaska is tundra. It is warm enough in southern Alaska for farmers to grow oats, barley, and potatoes.

Hawaii

Hawaii is farther west and farther south than any other state. It is hundreds of miles out in the Pacific Ocean. Hawaii is known for its mild, pleasant climate. Look at the top map. Find the islands of Hawaii.

 Look at the relief map of the islands of Hawaii. Compare it to the relief map of Alaska on page 136. How are the two states alike? Write your answer here.

_____

Hawaii's mountains are not like regular mountains. In fact, the islands of Hawaii were formed long ago by **volcanoes.** Volcanoes are openings in the crust of the earth through which melting rock, dust, ash, and hot gases are thrown up. The hot rock is called **lava.** When volcanoes **erupt,** they shoot lava into the air.

Millions of years ago, volcanoes under the Pacific Ocean erupted. The hardened lava formed the Hawaiian Islands. Even today, Hawaii's volcanoes erupt from time to time.

Some volcanoes in Hawaii still erupt from time to time. This photo shows some burning liquid lava flowing from a volcano.

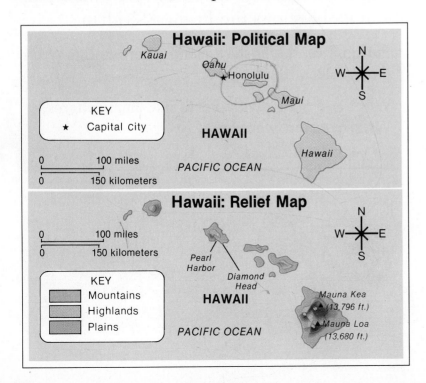

Hawaii: Political Map

Kauai

Oahu
★Honolulu

Maui

N
W—E
S

KEY
★ Capital city

HAWAII

0   100 miles
0   150 kilometers

PACIFIC OCEAN

Hawaii

Hawaii: Relief Map

0   100 miles
0   150 kilometers

Pearl
Harbor

Diamond
Head

N
W—E
S

KEY
Mountains
Highlands
Plains

HAWAII

PACIFIC OCEAN

Mauna Kea
▲ (13,796 ft.)

▲ Mauna Loa
(13,680 ft.)

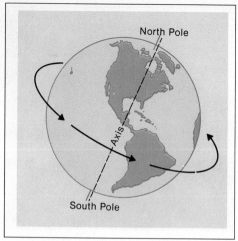

Earth spins on an imaginary axis. The North and South poles are the two ends of the axis.

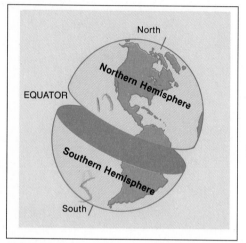

If we could cut Earth into a northern half and a southern half, it would look like this.

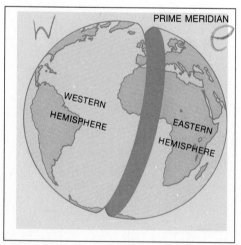

If we could cut Earth into an eastern half and a western half, it would look like this.

Dividing Earth

The Pacific Region states are spread over a large part of Earth. Look at the top globe on this page. Find the islands of Hawaii on the northern and western side of the globe.

How do we know where north or west is? Earth looks like a big ball, and a ball does not have a top or bottom. Look at the first globe again. Earth turns on an imaginary **axis,** or center line. The axis goes from the North Pole to the South Pole.

We divide Earth into a northern half and a southern half. These halves are called **hemispheres.** The imaginary line where the two halves meet is called the **Equator.** The globe in the middle shows the two hemispheres.

 Put an <u>N</u> on the Northern Hemisphere and an <u>S</u> on the Southern Hemisphere.

We also divide Earth into an Eastern Hemisphere and a Western Hemisphere. The line goes through the two big oceans.

The imaginary line between these hemispheres is called the **Prime Meridian.** The bottom globe shows the Prime Meridian.

 Put an <u>E</u> on the Eastern Hemisphere and a <u>W</u> on the Western Hemisphere.

What two lines divide Earth into hemispheres? Write your answers here.

Equator
Prime Meridian

UNIT PROJECT Tip

Write a climate report about your state. Tell visitors what clothes they should bring on a trip to your state. Would it be a good idea to pack an umbrella?

The people of Hawaii have come from many different places. People from Polynesia, Japan, Europe, China, and the Philippines have all settled in Hawaii. The first people who came to Hawaii were Polynesians.

Polynesia means "many islands." The islands of Polynesia are south of Hawaii. The names of some of the Polynesian islands are Tahiti, Tonga, and the Marquesas Islands.

This woman and girl are from Tahiti, which is part of Polynesia.

The most important thing to the Polynesians was the Pacific Ocean. They fished in large wooden boats that looked like double canoes. The Polynesians were very good sailors. They had no modern tools for finding their way on the ocean. They looked at patterns of stars to find their way.

The Polynesians were also great explorers. They discovered Hawaii. About 2,000 years ago, groups of Polynesians began settling Hawaii.

 Look at the map. Use the distance scale to find out about how many miles Tahiti is from Hawaii.

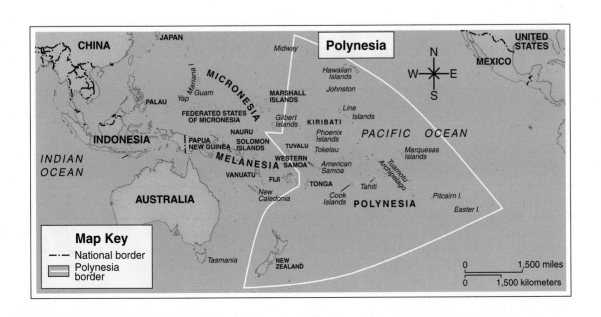

CHAPTER CHECKUP

Read each sentence. Circle the letter in front of the correct answer.

1. The West Coast states of the Pacific Region are
   a. California, Oregon, and Alaska.
   b. California, Oregon, and Washington.
   c. Oregon, Hawaii, and Alaska.
   d. Washington, Oregon, and Alaska.

2. Warm Pacific Ocean breezes help make the climate of the West Coast states
   a. cold.
   b. hot.
   c. dry.
   d. mild.

3. As wet air gets colder, it produces
   a. deserts.
   b. rain.
   c. sunshine.
   d. warm air.

4. The land in Alaska that is too cold to grow trees is called
   a. Canada.
   b. snow.
   c. tundra.
   d. a volcano.

5. The islands of Hawaii were formed by
   a. earthquakes.
   b. tourists.
   c. volcanoes.
   d. tundras.

6. The northern and southern halves of Earth are called the
   a. Prime Meridian.
   b. fault.
   c. hemispheres.
   d. axis.

 THINKING AND WRITING

Suppose you were going to move to Alaska or Hawaii. Which state would you choose? Explain your answer.

_____

_____

_____

_____

_____

People of the Pacific Region

Gold was discovered in California in 1848. People hurried there from all over. Here is a diary a gold hunter might have written.

Long Ago: The Gold Rush

20 October 1849 We finally got here, but it took us nearly four months. It was hard crossing the Rocky Mountains in a covered wagon. Our camp is called Rich Gulch. Many people are here already.

25 October 1849 My brother Jim and I got some land of our own. One man at Yuba River got 30 pounds of gold from his piece of land. So far we have only found a few dollars worth of gold. Everything costs a lot here.

24 November 1849 Most gold here is dust or tiny flakes. To find it, you put a handful of sand in a wash pan. Then you scoop up lots of water and move the pan in a circle to keep the sand moving. Gold is heavier, so it goes to the bottom. It is very hard work and we are not finding much gold.

2 February 1850 Today I came back from San Francisco with food and tools. Right away, people tried to buy them from me. People paid me in gold dust. I got more gold selling supplies than we found in the river in three months! Tomorrow we are going back to San Francisco to buy more supplies.

Why were so many people at Rich Gulch camp? Write your answer here.

Who Are the People of the Pacific Region?

The Pacific Region has as great a mixture of people and ways of life as you can find anywhere in the United States. People have moved to the region from all over the world. Many American Indians, Hispanics, and Asian Americans live in the Pacific Region.

American Indians came to the West Coast area thousands of years ago. Then Spanish colonists and Mexican Americans moved there. During the 1800s pioneers from the East began moving to the West. At that time the West was known as the **frontier.** A frontier is the farthest edge of a country, where few settlers live.

Most pioneers headed for California or Oregon. Pioneers gathered at Independence, Missouri, where trails to the California, Oregon, and Washington regions began. Back then the trails were really only tracks in the ground made by covered wagons that had traveled the trail earlier. The trip from Independence to Oregon on the Oregon Trail took six months! Large "trains" of covered wagons made the hard trip across deep rivers, deserts, and the Rocky Mountains. Often, the travelers ran out of food and water and got sick. Even though the trip was dangerous, by 1890 so much of the West had become settled that the United States government announced that the West was no longer a frontier.

Wagon trains usually included about 25 heavy wagons, each pulled by a team of 6 to 20 mules or oxen.

Why do you think pioneers wanted to make the hard journey to the West Coast?

_____

_____

_____

Many groups of American Indians, such as the Modoc and Yakima, lived near the West Coast. Before the settlers came, the American Indian groups fished, hunted, and used the trees of the forests to build boats and houses. The American Indians of the Pacific Region had many natural resources they could use.

When settlers and miners arrived, things changed. The settlers and the American Indians fought about how to use the land. Later, the government forced American Indian groups to go to reservations.

The Modoc was one group that fought against having to move to a reservation. But the government moved the Modoc to a reservation in Oregon. A chief named Kintpuash led a group of 80 families back to their old hunting grounds in California. The Army tried to force them back to the reservation. For five long months a small group of Modoc fought the soldiers. The Modoc finally lost the battle. They were moved to a reservation in Oklahoma.

The Yakima and many other Pacific Region American Indian groups still live in the West Coast states. Other American Indian groups such as the Inuit, Aleut, and Tlingit live in Alaska.

This picture shows how the Tlingit of Alaska lived long ago. Their large plank houses provided shelter for many related families.

Why do you think the Modoc went back to California? Write your answer here.

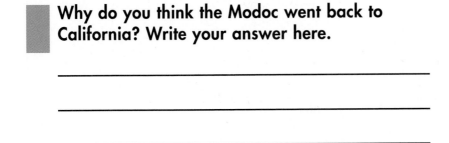

Thousands of settlers came to San Francisco, California, after gold was discovered in 1848. People in the late 1800s used cable cars to get up the hills of San Francisco. People still ride the cable cars today.

Remember that during the 1800s most immigrants to the eastern part of the United States came from countries in Europe. Immigrants from Europe came to the West too. They hoped to find gold or good land there. But immigration was also different in the West Coast area. In the middle of the 1800s, news of gold in California reached China. China is a country in Asia, which is across the Pacific Ocean. Immigrants from China came to California to look for gold. Because so many settlers were going west, railroad companies wanted to build railroads that would stretch all the way from the East Coast to the West Coast. Thousands of Chinese immigrants helped build the railroads.

 Look at the time line below. What was the first West Coast state?

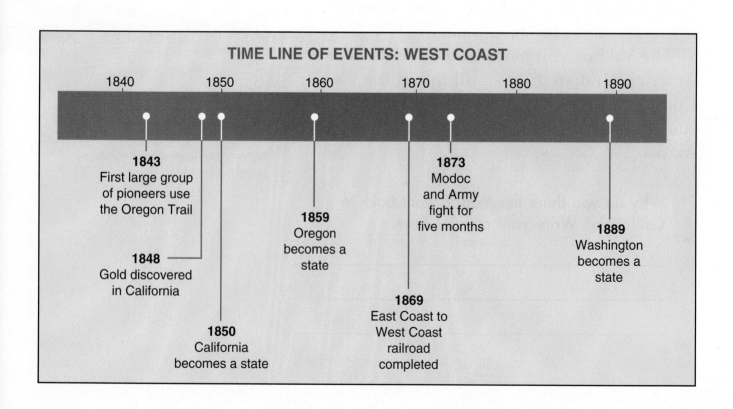

TIME LINE OF EVENTS: WEST COAST

1840   1850   1860   1870   1880   1890

1843
First large group of pioneers use the Oregon Trail

1848
Gold discovered in California

1850
California becomes a state

1859
Oregon becomes a state

1869
East Coast to West Coast railroad completed

1873
Modoc and Army fight for five months

1889
Washington becomes a state

Where Do People Live in the Pacific Region?

About 41 million people live in the Pacific Region. Alaska is our largest state, but few people live there. California has the biggest population in the country.

Why do you think Alaska has so few people?

_____

Besides the Pacific Region states, there are hundreds of Pacific Islands in the region. The United States has been closely tied to many of these islands, offering them aid and protection. Some, like the Marshall Islands, have since become independent nations. Others, like Guam, the Northern Marianas, and American Samoa, are U.S. territories.

Honolulu is the largest city in Hawaii. It has one of the best harbors in the world. Because it is in the middle of the Pacific Ocean, Honolulu has become a busy and important port. In the past, ships going to and from Asia stopped there for fresh water and food.

Honolulu is the capital of Hawaii.

145

The climate is very different in the states of the Pacific Region. (right) Anchorage, Alaska, is cold most of the year. (below) Southern California is warm all year round.

The city of Anchorage, Alaska, was once just a place where ships stopped. They were there to unload materials needed to build the Alaska Railroad. Today Anchorage is the largest city in Alaska.

Two of the most important West Coast ports are Portland, Oregon, and Seattle, Washington. Neither one of these ports is near the ocean. Portland is 100 miles up the Columbia River. Ships go there to pick up lumber and other products. Seattle is 125 miles from the ocean. It is not on a river but on a large bay called Puget Sound.

Los Angeles, California, is the largest city in the Pacific Region. It is known for its busy highways, its beautiful beaches, and Hollywood, the movie capital of the world.

 What are the names of three important ports in the Pacific Region? Write your answer here.

_____

_____

_____

Working in the Pacific Region

Look around your classroom. How many things do you see that are made of wood? Don't forget that paper is made from wood, too. The forests of Oregon and Washington provide many of the wood products we use.

The major product of Alaska is oil. The oil field in Alaska is bigger than any other in North America. A big pipeline carries the oil 800 miles from the northern part of Alaska to a harbor in southern Alaska. The pipeline is a very good way of transporting oil because roads cannot be built in the tundra areas of northern Alaska.

 What do you think happens to the oil when it reaches the harbor?

_____

_____

_____

After trees are cut down, the logs are taken to lumber mills where they are cut into boards.

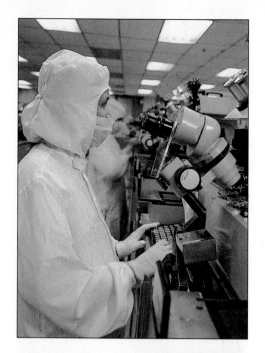

(top right) In most places in the United States, big machines plant and pick the crops. (top left) Workers and machines must be clean and free of dust at computer and software facilities. (bottom left) These tourists are enjoying the scenery of California. There are many national parks located throughout the Pacific Region.

More than half of all the fruits and vegetables you eat are grown in the West Coast states. California and Washington are also important centers for technology. Many large computer and software businesses are located in these two states.

Since all the states of the Pacific Region are near the Pacific Ocean, you have probably guessed that fishing is important. Service jobs are also very important. Many people in the region have jobs related to the tourism business. The Pacific Region is an area of great beauty. Each year, millions of people from all over the world visit the mountains, volcanoes, lakes, rivers, and exciting cities of the region.

 How is the Pacific Ocean a resource for the region?

UNIT PROJECT Tip Find out about some of the places that a visitor to your state would like to see. Collect photos of these places.

Maxine Hong Kingston

Readers across the United States discovered Maxine Hong Kingston when she wrote *Woman Warrior.* The book is about growing up in the Pacific Region. It also tells what life was like for women in China long ago. The stories in the book were stories that Kingston's mother told her when she was a child.

Later Kingston wrote another book about people in her family. But this time they were people she had never met. One was her great-grandfather, who moved from China to Hawaii. Another was a grandfather who came to California to help build the railroads. The book was called *China Men.*

Maxine Hong Kingston

Some of the events in both of these books really happened. Other events were taken from **myths,** or old stories. But whether they are real or made-up, the stories tell about Chinese American life in the Pacific Region.

Maxine Hong Kingston was a teacher before she became a writer. Her books have been published in many languages so people around the world can enjoy her writing.

Imagine that you are a writer from the Pacific Region. Which group of people do you think you would like to write about?

_____

_____

_____

Complete each sentence. Circle the letter in front of the correct answer.

1. In the middle 1800s, people rushed to California to find

   a. trees.
   b. houses.
   c. gold.
   d. fruit.

2. The farthest edge of a country where few settlers live is the

   a. West Coast.
   b. frontier.
   c. Pacific region.
   d. tundra.

3. Chinese immigrants helped build a

   a. gold mine.
   b. wagon trail.
   c. pipeline for oil.
   d. coast-to-coast railroad.

4. The largest city in Hawaii is

   a. San Francisco.
   b. Honolulu.
   c. Hawaii City.
   d. Anchorage.

5. Many of the Pacific Region's biggest cities are

   a. important ports.
   b. in the Central Valley.
   c. not near water.
   d. in Hawaii.

6. The largest oil field in North America is in

   a. Texas.
   b. Puget Sound.
   c. California.
   d. Alaska.

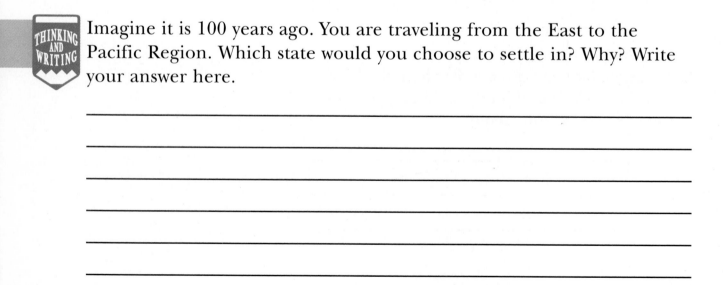

THINKING AND WRITING Imagine it is 100 years ago. You are traveling from the East to the Pacific Region. Which state would you choose to settle in? Why? Write your answer here.

_____

_____

_____

_____

_____

FACTS ABOUT THE STATES OF THE PACIFIC REGION

STATE Origin of Name *Nickname(s)*	Capital	Population *(estimate)*	Rank	Bird	Flower
Alaska Word comes from the way Russian settlers said the Aleutian islanders' word for "mainland." *Last Frontier* *Land of the Midnight Sun*	Juneau	599,000	**Pop**. 49 **Size** 1	Willow ptarmigan	Forget-me-not
California Named by Spanish explorers for a treasure island in a Spanish story. *Golden State*	Sacramento	31,211,000	**Pop**. 1 **Size** 3	California valley quail	Golden poppy
Hawaii Named by early Polynesians for the place they came from. *Aloha State*	Honolulu	1,172,000	**Pop**. 40 **Size** 47	Nene (Hawaiian goose)	Hibiscus
Oregon French name for the Columbia River was *Ouragan,* which means "hurricane." *Beaver State*	Salem	3,038,000	**Pop**. 29 **Size** 10	Western meadowlark	Oregon grape
Washington Named for George Washington. *Evergreen State* *Chinook State*	Olympia	5,255,000	**Pop**. 18 **Size** 20	Willow goldfinch	Coast rhododendron

Learning from a Diagram

What causes a volcano to erupt? Very deep down in the earth there is melted rock called **magma.** During a volcanic eruption, the magma is pushed up through weaker rocks around it. When it reaches the surface of the earth, it is called lava. The diagram below shows you what a volcano would look like if it were cut in half.

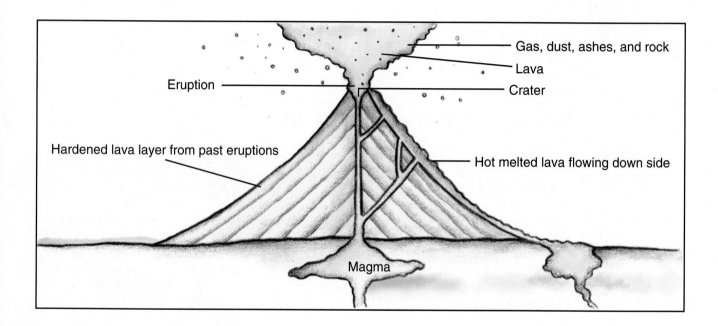

Gas, dust, ashes, and rock

Lava

Eruption

Crater

Hardened lava layer from past eruptions

Hot melted lava flowing down side

Magma

1. What is the bowl-shaped top of the volcano?

_____

2. What are the sides of the volcano made of?

_____

3. Trace one path of the magma to the surface.

4. Describe what you think it would be like to see a volcano erupt.

_____

_____

Now it's time to finish your unit project. Think about what you learned about the state your team studied. Talk with your team about answers to questions like these.

- **What is the climate like in the state?**

- **What are some interesting places to visit?**

Decide how to show the results of your team's project. Use one of the ideas below or an idea of your own.

➤ Publish a travel guide about your state. Include tips about climate and weather. Write captions for the photos you collected. Display your travel guides in the classroom.

➤ Use your climate report and photos to plan an advertising campaign for your state. Show people why they should visit the state. Tell them what fun they would have in the state. Make a magazine ad or a TV commercial.

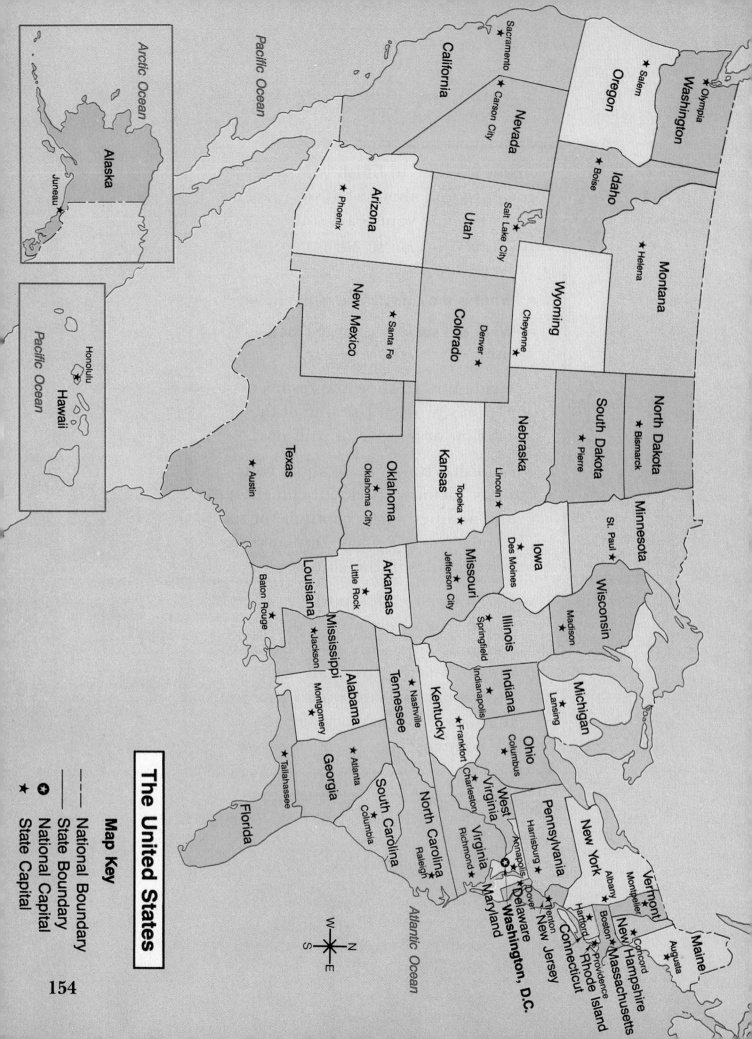

The United States

Map Key

- - - - National Boundary
———— State Boundary
⊛ National Capital
★ State Capital

154

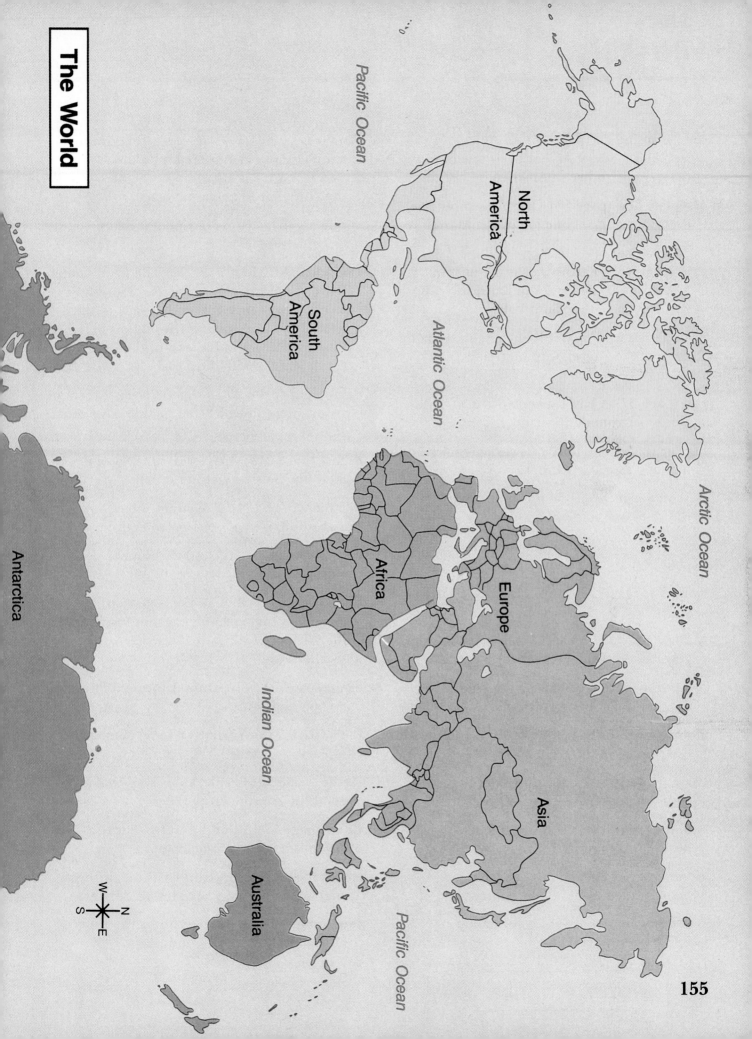

The World

North America

South America

Pacific Ocean

Atlantic Ocean

Arctic Ocean

Africa

Europe

Asia

Indian Ocean

Pacific Ocean

Antarctica

Australia

N
W E
S

Glossary

American Indian (page 16) An American Indian, or Native American, is one of the first people to live in America.

assembly line (page 85) On an assembly line, each worker does one job over and over again.

axis (page 138) Earth's axis is the imaginary line through the center of Earth from the North Pole to the South Pole.

basin (page 97) A basin is an area of low land shaped like a bowl, with high sides all around.

bay (page 37) A bay is a body of water that is almost surrounded by land.

border (page 6) A border is an imaginary line between states or nations.

boycott (page 127) When people boycott, they refuse to buy something.

canal (page 77) A canal is a waterway built by people that links bodies of water.

canyon (page 97) A canyon is a deep, narrow valley.

capital (page 35) A capital is the city where government leaders meet.

climate (page 12) Climate is the kind of weather a place has over time.

climate map (page 12) A climate map shows the climate in different areas.

coast (page 10) A coast is the land that runs along the ocean.

colonist (page 17) A colonist is a person who lives in a colony.

colony (page 17) A colony is a land and people ruled by another country.

communicate (page 46) To communicate is to share information.

Congress (page 25) Congress is the group of people who make the nation's laws. The U.S. Congress is made up of the Senate and the House of Representatives.

continent (page 6) A continent is a large body of land.

Continental Divide (page 96) The Continental Divide is an imaginary line through the Rocky Mountains. Rivers that start to the west of the Continental Divide flow west. Rivers that start to the east of the Continental Divide flow east.

democracy (page 25) A democracy is a form of government in which the people have equal rights and choose their own leaders.

desert (page 115) A desert is an area of dry land that gets very little rainfall.

diagram (page 134) A diagram shows how something is made or how something works.

earthquake (page 135) An earthquake is a strong shaking of the ground.

Equator (page 138) The Equator is an imaginary line around the middle of Earth that divides Earth into a northern and a southern half.

erupt (page 137) To erupt is to shoot lava into the air, as a volcano does.

fault (page 135) A fault is a long, deep break in Earth's surface.

fertile (page 57) Fertile soil is land that is good for growing crops.

flood (page 57) A flood is water that rises and covers land that is usually dry.

frontier (page 142) A frontier is the farthest edge of a country, where few settlers live.

geography (page 6) Geography is the study of Earth and how we live on it.

glacier (page 97) A glacier is a huge field of ice and snow.

government (page 24) A government is a group of people who make the rules and lead others in towns, cities, states, and countries.

governor (page 25) A governor is a person who leads a state.

gulf (page 55) A gulf is a large body of water that lies along a coast and joins an ocean.

harbor (page 37) A harbor is an area of water that is protected by land from wind and strong waves.

hemisphere (page 138) A hemisphere is one half of Earth.

highland (page 36) A highland is hilly land between flat land and mountains.

homesteading (page 80) Homesteading is living and working on land given by the government.

House of Representatives (page 25) The House of Representatives is a part of Congress. The number of members depends on the population of their states.

hurricane (page 55) A hurricane is a storm with very strong winds and heavy rain.

immigrant (page 19) An immigrant is a person who leaves one country to live in another.

irrigation (page 115) Irrigation is watering crops by bringing water to an area where it is in short supply.

labor union (page 127) A labor union is a group of workers who try to get better working conditions and pay for its members.

landform (page 10) A landform is a shape of the land, such as a mountain or hill.

lava (page 137) Lava is hot, melted rock from inside a volcano.

law (page 24) A law is a rule made by a government.

line graph (page 103) A line graph uses lines to show how something changes over time.

local government (page 24) A local government is a group of people who make the laws and lead the people of a town or city.

manufacturing (page 46) Manufacturing is making goods.

mayor (page 25) A mayor is a person who leads a town or city.

miner (page 103) A miner is a person who digs for minerals in the earth.

mineral (page 27) A mineral is something made by nature that is found in the earth. Silver is a mineral.

moisture (page 12) Moisture is how wet the air is.

Mormons (page 104) The Mormons are a religious group who went to Utah to find land and a place to worship.

myth (page 149) A myth is a story that tells about history and what people believe.

Native American (page 16) A Native American is an American Indian, one of the first people to live in America.

natural resource (page 27) A natural resource is something from nature that people need and use.

pioneer (page 80) A pioneer is a person who goes to live in a new place.

plain (page 10) A plain is a low, flat area of land.

plantation (page 64) A plantation is a very large farm.

plateau (page 10) A plateau is a high, flat area of land.

population (page 82) Population is the number of people who live in a place.

port (page 37) A port is a place where ships can load and unload goods.

prairie (page 76) A prairie is a large area of land with grass but few trees.

predict (page 14) To predict is to tell what will probably happen.

President (page 25) The President is the person who leads the country.

Prime Meridian (page 138) The Prime Meridian is an imaginary line that runs north and south and divides Earth into an eastern and a western half.

province (page 47) A province is a division of a country. In Canada, provinces are like states in the United States.

recycle (page 27) To recycle is to reuse resources in order to keep from running out of those resources.

refinery (page 126) A refinery is a place where oil is cleaned and separated into different products.

region (page 8) A region is an area that land is divided into for study.

relief map (page 10) A relief map gives information about types and shapes of land such as mountains and plains.

research (page 126) Research means studying things to find out about them.

reservation (page 102) A reservation is land set aside by the government where American Indian groups can live.

rodeo (page 104) A rodeo is a contest for cowboys and cowgirls.

route (page 75) A route is a way or plan of travel to take from one place to another.

satellite (page 14) A satellite is something sent from Earth into space, usually to gather information.

Senate (page 25) The Senate is a part of Congress. There are two members from each state in the Senate.

service (page 24) A service is something that helps people.

service job (page 26) A service job is a job in which people do something to help other people.

settler (page 101) A settler is a person who goes to live in a new part of a country.

slave (page 19) A slave is a person who is owned by another person.

sod (page 81) Sod is blocks of dirt with grass growing in them.

solar energy (page 126) *Solar energy* means using the heat of the sun.

special-purpose map (page 10) A special-purpose map gives special facts about just one topic.

strike (page 127) A strike is the stopping of work by the workers.

suburb (page 42) A suburb is a small town or city that is near a big city.

Sunbelt (page 62) The Sunbelt is part of the southern United States, where it is usually warm and sunny.

swamp (page 57) A swamp is an area of soft land that is always wet.

temperature (page 12) Temperature is how hot or cold the air is.

transportation (page 42) Transportation is how people or goods travel from one place to another.

tundra (page 136) A tundra is a cold, treeless area where the ground is almost always frozen.

united (page 6) *United* means together.

United Nations (page 38) The United Nations is a group of many countries that works to try to solve problems.

volcano (page 137) A volcano is an opening in the crust of the earth through which melting rock, dust, ash, and hot gases are thrown up.

vote (page 25) To vote is to make a choice.

weather (page 12) Weather is how hot or cold it is. Moisture is also part of weather.

Index